UNIVERSITY MEETS MICROFINANCE AWARDS

University Meets Microfinance (UMM) presents its tenth "UMM Award":

Each year, in order to foster research in topics related to financial inclusion and give recognition to the work of young researchers, UMM rewards and publishes outstanding students' research in this domain. The UMM Award winners are selected by a Selection Committee composed by qualified professors and practitioners.

Nicole Tode, Master student from Goethe Universität Frankfurt has been awarded in 2012 for her thesis on "*Transforming Microfinance Institutions: A possible way to go for Moroccan Microcredit Associations*".

We want to especially thank the following Selection Committee members for their participation in 2012 UMM Awards selection process:

Academics: Thorsten Beck (Tilburg University); Vincenzo Provenzano (University of Palermo); Ahmad Nawaz (Universität Göttingen); Ariane Szafarz, Marek Hudon and Jessica Schicks (Université Libre de Bruxelles); Fernando Rodriguez (Universidad de Salamanca); Luciano Bonomo and Simonetta Chiodi (Università degli Studi di Bergamo); Margherita Mori (Università degli Studi dell'Aquila); Roberto Moro Visconti (Cattolica University Milano); Oliver Gloede (Leibniz Universität Hannover); Thilo Klein (University of Cambridge); Ursula Stiegler (Freie Universität Berlin)

Practitioners: Daniela Pensotti, David Levai, Didier Krumm, Eliane Augareils, Frances Fraser, Gabrielle Harris, Maud Chalamet and Vanessa Quintero (PlaNet Finance); Florent Bédécarrats (CERISE); Hans Jörg Kessler (FIDES); Katja Kirchstein (A leading association of the German banking industry); Maria Alejandra Guglielmetti (Capgemini Italia); Maud Savary-Mornet (PlaNIS responsAbility SAS); Philippe Guichandut (Grameen Crédit Agricole Foundation); Roland Knorren (Consultant to ACCION); Sébastien Weber (PlaNet Guarantee)

This publication has been made possible thanks to the financial support of:

PlaNet Finance

European Microfinance Platform

With the financial support of BMZ Federal Ministry for Economic Cooperation and Development

giz Deutsche Gesellschaft für Internationale Zusammenarbeit (GIZ) GmbH

Frankfurt School of Finance & Management Bankakademie | HfB

Capgemini Consulting.Technology.Outsourcing

escem

Sogeti

UNIVERSITY MEETS MICROFINANCE

edited by PlaNet Finance Deutschland e.V.

ISSN 2190-2291

The growing interest by students and academics as well as the increasing need for knowledge creation and dissemination in the microfinance sector, led to the launch of University Meets Microfinance (UMM) by PlaNet Finance and Freie Universität Berlin in 2009.

UMM is a European initiative which fosters the cooperation between universities, students in Europe and microfinance practitioners to contribute to microfinance innovation and education for development. UMM is active in the domains of microfinance education, microfinance research, capitalization of information, professional exchange & dissemination of information. All UMM activities are carried out under the umbrella of the European Microfinance Platform (e-MFP) in the frame of the e-MFP UMM Action Group.

Up to 2012, more than 2.200 students, academics and practitioners have benefitted from UMM activities.

CONTACT AND FOLLOW UMM:

www.universitymeetsmicrofinance.eu
www.e-mfp.eu/action-groups/university-meets-microfinance
umm@planetfinance.org
www.facebook.com/universitymeetsmicrofinance

Volumes

8 *Anna Custers*
Furthering Financial Literacy
Experimental Evidence from a Financial Literacy Training Programme for Microfinance Clients in Bhopal, India
ISBN 978-3-8382-0337-9

9 *Thilo Klein*
Why Do India's Urban Poor Choose to Go Private?
Health Policy Simulations in Slums of Hyderabad
ISBN 978-3-8382-0238-9

10 *Nicole Tode*
Transforming Microfinance Institutions
A possible way to go for Moroccan Microcredit Associations
ISBN 978-3-8382-0494-9

Nicole Tode

TRANSFORMING MICROFINANCE INSTITUTIONS

A possible way to go for Moroccan Microcredit Associations

ibidem-Verlag
Stuttgart

Bibliografische Information der Deutschen Nationalbibliothek
Die Deutsche Nationalbibliothek verzeichnet diese Publikation in der Deutschen Nationalbibliografie; detaillierte bibliografische Daten sind im Internet über http://dnb.d-nb.de abrufbar.

Bibliographic information published by the Deutsche Nationalbibliothek
Die Deutsche Nationalbibliothek lists this publication in the Deutsche Nationalbibliografie; detailed bibliographic data are available in the Internet at http://dnb.d-nb.de.

∞

Gedruckt auf alterungsbeständigem, säurefreien Papier
Printed on acid-free paper

ISSN: 2190-2291

ISBN-13: 978-3-8382-0494-9

Printed in Germany

Foreword

As it is generally perceived, microfinance is a relatively new phenomenon, although its precursors have existed since decades, if not even centuries. The vague term microfinance refers to the provision of small and very small - or micro - loans and other financial services to small and very small - or micro - businesses and other people of limited means, who typically have so far not had access to the services of existing banks and other formal financial institutions. At the latest, microfinance has become known worldwide in 2006 when Professor Muhammad Yunus from Bangladesh and Grameen Bank, the bank for poor people he had founded in the 1970s, were jointly awarded the Noble Peace Price for their effort to create economic and social development from below by making small loans available to women who had so far not had access to loans except those from usurious money lenders.

The Noble Peace Price was well deserved, because microfinance can be assumed to be an effective instrument to combat poverty, and abject and wide-spread poverty is indeed a threat to peace in a country and even beyond. As an organization that does highly effective and indeed also very efficient social work, the Grameen Bank is indeed a model. However, as a microfinance institution it is not beyond all critique and it is certainly not a model for other microfinance institutions. At least for quite some time, its business model was unusual and almost impossible for others to imitate. It consisted in the Bank doing good work whose costs were higher than its revenue and in having Yunus as a charismatic personality and a very gifted public speaker who travelled the capital cities of this world to raise the funds needed to cover the considerable deficits.

Hundreds of other microfinance institutions all over the world were not in a position to follow this model, since they did not have a speaker and fundraiser like Yunus, and therefore they had to find other ways of making ends meet. A conceptually simple alternative for microfinance institutions is to keep their costs really low and to charge their clients interest rates that are moderate but sufficient to cover costs and achieve financial sustainability. This strategy has been called the commercial approach to microfinance. Microfinance institutions can have various institutional forms. For one that has adopted the commercial approach, the natural choice is that of a licensed bank in the legal form of a corporation with public as well as private entities as shareholders. Since most microfinance institutions have for many years been organized as foundations, associations and the like, that is, as credit-granting NGOs, transforming into a corporation and at the same time into a licensed bank is a huge step. But this step, which is called upgrading in the development jargon, has been made successfully by a number of microfinance institutions in countries where the legal system allowed this transformation.

In Morroco, this has for a long time not been possible. In spite of several restrictions, microfinance in Morocco had developed quite strongly at least until 2007. There are a few microfinance NGOs in this country that command high respect among experts. Recent legal changes have now made upgrading or transforming them possible and this raises the almost natural questions, how this can be done, what the required preconditions are and finally whether it is a good idea for leading Moroccan microfinance institutions to make this huge step.

Ms. Tode has addressed this important and timely question in her Master Thesis written at my chair for international banking at the Goethe University in Frankfurt. Her thesis is a highly original and very diligent piece of research. Ms. Tode has collected a lot of information about the microfinance landscape in Morocco, about the leading microfinance NGOs, which are possible candidates for upgrading or transformation, and about the pre- and post-transformation performance of a number of Latin American microfinance institutions that have adopted the corporate form and have put themselves under normal bank regulation. Comparing the data for the Moroccan and the Latin American institutions, she has been able to show that for the best Moroccan microfinance NGOs, but only for them, it is certainly worth considering a transformation, even though she avoids to simply recommend making this step.

The result of her study is as well founded as the entire study. Being duly cautious in her final conclusion is one of the numerous strengths of Ms. Todes work, which is highly instructive reading for anyone who is interested in microfinance in Morroco and upgrading of microfinance NGOs in general.

I cordially congratulate Nicole Tode to having received and in my view truly deserved a prestigious prize for her work, and I am really proud of her since after all she is one of our cherished students. It is great that her thesis will now be published and thereby becomes accessible for many interested readers.

Reinhard H. Schmidt
Goethe-University, Frankfurt, 28.2.2013

Contents

List of Tables

List of Figures

List of Abbrevations

List of Abbreviations

ACLEDA	Association of Cambodian Local Economic Development Agencies
ADEMI	Association for the Development of Microenterprises
ADOPEM	Asociación Dominicana para el Desarrollo de la Mujer (Microfinance Bank providing loans to women)
AMPES	Asociación de Medianos y Pequeños Empresarios de El Salvador (Association providing loans to small and medium-sized enterprises)
ATM	Automated Teller Machine
BaFin	Bundesanstalt für Finanzdienstleistungsaufsicht (German Federal Financial Supervisory Authority)
BAM	Banque Al Maghrib (Al Maghrib Bank)
BANEX	Banco del Exito (Nicaraguan Microfinance Institution)
BIO	Belgian Investment Company for Developing Countries
CGAP	Consultative Group to Assist the Poor
CLA	Caja Los Andes (Bolivian Microfinance Institution)
DOEN	Stichting Duurzame Ontwikkeling En Natuurbescherming (Foundation for sustainable development and nature conservation, Netherlands)
EECA	Eastern Europe and Central Asia
EIB	European Investment Bank

FBPMC	Fondation Banque Populaire Microcredit (Microcredit Foundation Banque Populaire)
FFP	Fondo Financiero Privado (Private Financial Fund)
FI	Financial Institution
FINDESA	Nicaragüense de Desarrollo Sociedad Anónima (Nicaraguan Development Corporation)
FMO	Financierings-Maatschappij voor Ontwikkelingslanden (Netherlands Development Finance Company)
FNAM	Fédération Nationale des Associations de Microcrédit (National Federation of Microcredit Associations)
FONDEP	Fondation pour le Développement Local et le Partenariat (Foundation for the Local Development and Partnership)
GDP	Gross Domestic Product
GIZ	Gesellschaft für Internationale Zusammenarbeit (German Agency for International Cooperation)
GNI	Gross National Income
IFC	International Finance Corporation
IFRS	International Financial Reporting Standards
ILO	International Labour Organization
IMF	International Monetary Fund
IMI	Internationale Micro Investitionen AG (Private institution for investments in microfinance banks)
IPC	International Project Consult
IPO	Initial Public Offering
JB	Jarque-Bera test
KfW	Kreditanstalt für Wiederaufbau (German Development Bank)
LAC	Latin America and the Caribbean
MAD	Moroccan Dirham
MCA	Microcredit Association
MENA	Middle East and Northern Africa
MFB	Microfinance Bank
MFI	Microfinance Institution

MIX	Microfinance Information Exchange
NBFI	Non-Bank Financial Institution
NGO	Non-Governmental Organization
NRDSC	Nepal Rural Development Society Centre
OECD	Organization for Economic Cooperation and Development
OSS	Operational Self-sufficiency
PAR	Portfolio at Risk
PCB	ProCredit Bank
PCH	ProCredit Holding
PRODEM	Fundación para la Promoción y el Desarrollo de la Microempresa (Foundation for the Promotion and Development of Microenterprises)
ROA	Return on Assets
ROE	Return on Equity
UNDP	United Nations Development Programme
USAID	United States Agency for International Development
USD	United States Dollar

1 Introduction

Microfinance institutions (MFI) focus on providing credits to poor people who otherwise have no access to formal financial services (Hermes *et al.*, 2008). MFIs intend to reduce poverty by supporting the poor with setting up their own income generating businesses. Due to its charitable character, this focus is generally described as outreach in the microfinance industry. However, providing credit to poor people is a very costly activity as it implies high administrative and monitoring costs. Thus, a high outreach can conflict with the financial sustainability of the MFIs. International donor agencies and commercial banks provide financial support to the MFIs by offering loans with favourable conditions. They support the MFIs in lending to domestic small companies and poor individuals. Recently there has been a shift from subsidizing MFIs to become financial sustainable and efficient institutions. This often leads to a change in the MFIs' behaviour, broadening their services and activities (Hermes *et al.*, 2008). One typical change is the institutional transformation of MFIs from a Non-Governmental Organization (NGO) into a regulated Microfinance Bank (MFB). Currently this is a major issue for the Moroccan Microcredit Associations (MCA). Morocco has the best performing MFIs in the Arab world (Reille, 2010, 2009). Moreover, the Moroccan microfinance sector is the most advanced and developed sector in the Middle East and Northern Africa (MENA) region (Reille, 2010). According to Atallah and El Hyani (2009) the institutional transformation of the MCAs is necessary to adequately meet the existing demand for microfinance services in Morocco. There are three MCAs in particular, Al Amana, FONDEP, and FBPMC, which are the largest institutions in the Moroccan microfinance sector and thus have the potential to transform into regulated MFBs (Allaire *et al.*, 2009). In order to assess their future development, the following questions will be answered in this thesis:

1. *How will these institutions develop over time?*
2. *Are conditions and requirements sufficiently met?*
3. *Is such a transformation advantageous for the MCAs?*

This study is structured as follows: In the first section, the theoretical background and methodology are outlined, including relevant literature, data resources and the course of the study. Chapter 3 describes the Moroccan financial system and microfinance sector. This chapter also includes the profiles of the major MCAs and three selected transformed MFBs. Chapter 4 comprises two comparative analyses that compare the institutions before and after their institutional transformation. It provides a detailed description of the potentials and the requirements faced by the MCAs. Finally, the conclusion summarizes the results of this thesis.

The data and information included in this masters thesis are accurate and complete up to the point of completion of my work in March 2012. Events and legal changes that occurred after that date could not be taken into account.

2 Theoretical Background and Methodology

Relevant literature

Over the past thirty years, the microfinance sector has undergone various changes as more and more MFIs that used to be run as NGOs have started to change their legal status (Fernando, 2004; Quayes, 2011). Up until the 1980s microcredit was largely operated by NGOs and state-sponsored programs. They began microcredit operations because conventional Financial Institutions (FI) did not provide financial services to poor people, low-income households, and their microenterprises. This changed, as NGOs increased their outreach and therefore transformed into regulated MFIs in various countries, mainly in Latin-America and Asia. In 1992 the former PRODEM NGO in Bolivia was the first MFI to change its status into a formal bank, named BancoSol (Fernando, 2004; Quayes, 2011). Several authors describe this commercialization of MFIs as increased focus on sustainability (Hermes *et al.*, 2008; Rhyne and Otero, 2006; Hartarska and Nadolnyak, 2007; Pollinger *et al.*, 2007; Cull *et al.*, 2009). During the last three decades some shareholder-owned, regulated MFIs have provided a wide range of financial services to poor and low-income individuals (Fernando, 2004). They expected to increase the depth and scope of their outreach mainly through improved access to commercial sources of funds and public deposits. However, the number of such MFIs remains low. Even so, the MFIs' overall influence and effect on the industry are relatively high considering their position in the industry (Fernando, 2004).

The term *MFI* is defined as an organization that provides financial services to poor people. The definition includes a wide range of providers that vary in their legal structure, mission, and methodology. However, all institutions share the characteristic of providing financial services to clients who are poorer and more vulnerable than traditional bank clients (CGAP, 2011).

MFIs can have different legal forms. They can be savings and loan cooperatives, loan unions, government banks, commercial banks, Non-Bank Financial Institutions (NBFI) or NGOs (Ledgerwood, 1998). A *NGO* is an organization registered as a non-profit for tax purposes or some other legal form. Its financial services are more restricted and typically do not include savings products. They are usually not regulated by a banking supervisory authority (MIXMarket, 2010). The Moroccan MFIs have a legal NGO status. They are also called Microcredit Associations (MCA), derived from the French terminus *Associations de Microcrédit* (Atallah and El Hyani, 2009; JAÏDA, 2011). The term *Microcredit Association* indicates that the organization already commits to certain regulations and is therefore recognized by the *Ministry of the Economy and Finance* in Morocco (see also Appendix C) (Allaire *et al.*, 2009; Reille and Lyman, 2005; IMF, 2008).

Some NGOs intend to transform into regulated FIs or NBFIs before they become a MFB. A *NBFI* is defined as an institution that provides similar services as a bank but is licensed under a separate category. The separate license can result in lower capital requirements, limitations on financial service offerings, or supervision under a different state agency (MIXMarket, 2010).
In this context, a *bank* or a MFB is described as a licensed financial intermediary regulated by a state banking supervisory agency. It can provide any number of financial services, including savings products, loans, payment services, and money transfers (MIXMarket, 2010). MFBs are also established to provide financial services to people who would otherwise be excluded from the existing, formal financial sector (Jegede *et al.*, 2011).

Finally, an *institutional transformation* in the context of microfinance is defined as the establishment of a regulated FI by a NGO or a group of NGOs. The NGO's loan portfolio is totally or partially transferred to the new formal institution. However, it is possible that the NGO coexists alongside the newly established FI. Such was the case of PRODEM in Bolivia, which continued its operations after the foundation of BancoSol. Later in 1999 the NGO PRODEM was also transformed into another FI named FFP PRODEM (Fernando, 2004; Campion and White, 2001). Thus, an existing NGO which converts into a MFB can either incorporate a subsidiary MFB while still carrying out its NGO operations, or fully transform into a MFB (Okojie *et al.*, 2009).

In the context of MFI transformation, Terberger (2003) compares three ways of MFI building and transformation. The methods are called *up-scaling* (MFIs becoming formal banks specializing in microfinance), *downscaling* (introducing microcredit departments in existing, formal FIs), and the *green-field method* (possessing a banking licence from the very outset). Terberger (2003) states that the concept of for-profit microfinance, as well as the founding of greenfield banks, seeks to develop the financial market by reaching new customers. Moreover, Schmidt and Winkler (2000) shows evidence why building up financial institutions can be problematic in developing countries. One reason are the inappropriate expectations of donor and partner institutions regarding the problems and effects of institution building efforts. A second one is the lack of awareness of the importance of governance and ownership structures. Finally, existing financial regulations may be too restrictive for microfinance operations (Schmidt and Winkler, 2000). Hishigsuren (2006) presents an overview of the transformation experience in the area of microfinance. This article shows key issues and challenges (e. g. organizational structure, client transitioning, and competition) before, during, and after the institutional transformation. The paper proposes a tool that helps managers of NGOs to assess their situation and decide whether or not to transform, and if so, how. Similar outcomes are explored by Campion and White (2001), and Campion and White (1999).

After describing how MFIs can be built up, the study of Fernando (2004) analyses the success of already transformed MFIs located in different countries. Fernando (2004) shows that many of these institutions have been able to achieve positive results in four areas: new ownership structure with shareholders, increased access to commercial sources, wider range of services including savings products, and increased outreach (Fernando, 2004). Amha (2004) also shows that MFIs in Ethiopia reached different goals in the process of MFI commercialization. The institutions achieved higher outreach in terms of clients, loans, and savings products. Amha (2004) demonstrates that MFIs in Ethiopia were capable to reduce their Portfolio at Risk (PAR) values as well (Amha, 2004). Besides other studies, Jansson (2003) states that especially the Latin-American microfinance industry is undergoing rapid change. The number of specialized formal MFIs is rising rapidly due to the reconstitution or transformation of non-profit foundations. The new institutions are growing fast, and they need funds to support their growth. Since their regulation, MFIs have many different options to fund themselves. However, they are also under greater pressure to correctly manage currencies and term-structures in their balance sheets (Jansson, 2003). Moreover, Hartarska and Nadolnyak (2007) analyses the impact of regulation on MFI performance. The authors provide an overview how regulated MFIs perform in contrast to non-regulated MFIs. The main findings are that regulatory involvement does not directly affect performance either in terms of operational self-sustainability (cost covering) or outreach. They are also not likely to be more financially sustainable or reach more poor borrowers than MFIs who remain unregulated. However, the study shows that better capitalized as well as less leveraged MFIs are more sustainable. In addition, regulated MFIs which are collecting savings achieve better outreach because regulation is the only way for the MFIs to access savings from the public (Hartarska and Nadolnyak, 2007).

To conclude, research and literature capturing the development of MFIs' transformations often describe the advantages of such transformed institutions, i.e. increased outreach, better financial performance, and access to new funding sources. One can hence assume that the ongoing transformation process of the Moroccan MCAs can be advantageous for the institutions and their stakeholders, such as their clients and the Moroccan government (tax payments). Taking into account the experience from other transformed MFIs, it is possible to assess the MCAs' institutional development after their transformation.

Data resources

This thesis presents an analysis of data from multiple sources. One is the *New Database on Financial Development and Structure*, which was updated in November 2010. This is a database with indicators of financial development and structure across countries and over time. The indicators measure the size, activity, and efficiency of financial intermediaries and markets (Beck *et al.*, 2000, 2010).

Data on the microfinance industry is available from the Microfinance Information Exchange (MIX) dataset (MIXMarket, 2010). This is a web-based platform that contains extensive financial and outreach information for MFIs. The MFIs add data from their financial statements and outreach reports to the MIX dataset. MIX converts the individual local currency values into United States Dollar (USD) amounts by using the prevailing exchange rate. Afterwards they transform the data provided into a list of standardized financial and outreach variables which can be publicly requested (Quayes, 2011). The dataset provides data from over 2,000 MFIs out of an estimated number of over 10,000 MFIs worldwide (Hartarska *et al.*, 2011). The MIX dataset is purely self-reported and voluntary. However, all MIX data is verified by their analysts and reclassified to comply with the International Financial Reporting Standards (IFRS). It is a relatively large database and represents a vast majority of the total amount of MFIs in the world (Allaire *et al.*, 2009; Hartarska and Nadolnyak, 2007).

Unpublished data was provided by some of the MFIs described in this study.

The ProCredit Banks (PCB) in El Salvador and Bolivia contributed financial and operational data. Moreover, information on the PCBs' development was communicated with employees from the PCB in Germany (see Chapter 4.2.1). Furthermore, ACLEDA Bank in Cambodia and the Moroccan MCAs also provided data exclusively for the purpose of this thesis. ACLEDA Bank sent two presentations with information on their transformation process, i.e. general requirements and achievements. One of the MCAs provided a loan dataset which is comparable to the one of the PCBs. Finally, a list of MFIs with legal status transitions was sent from the MIX Market organization in Washington, DC.

Course of the study

The analysis of transformed MFIs carried out in this thesis aims to describe one possible future path of development of the MCAs. As stated in Fernando (2004), MFIs in Asia and the Latin America and the Caribbean (LAC) region were the first NGOs worldwide to transform into regulated MFIs. Their institutional data represents the whole institutional development of the transformation processes.

The analysis part of this thesis is split into two comparative analyses of the institutions in question, both before and after their transformation. In the first part of the analysis, the MCAs are compared to four NGOs before the institutional transformation of the latter. The aim is to see if the Moroccan institutions experienced the same developments as former NGOs did or if they completely differ e. g. in terms of institutional size or financial performance (see Chapter 4.1.1). The following subsection outlines the discussion about transforming MFIs and the major advantages and disadvantagessuch a transition of legal status incurs (see Chapter 4.1.2). The second part of the analysis compares the PCBs and 16 MFBs after their institutional transformation by means of different indicators. The objective is to establish whether the MFBs experienced similar institutional developments after their transformation or not (see Chapter 4.2.1). If the institutions' experiences are similar, their data can be applicable to describe the possible development of the Moroccan MCAs.

The 16 MFBs are selected out of a total sample of 108 institutions which are listed as a *bank* in the MIX dataset[1]. After checking the development history of these 108 banks, 16 banks were identified as former NGOs. These banks are: Caja Social BCSC and Bancamía S.A. in Colombia; MiBanco in Peru; Banco ADOPEM and Banco ADEMI located in the Dominican Republic; BancoSol in Bolivia; K-Rep bank in Kenya; D-Miro in Ecuador; Banco FIE in Bolivia; Nirdhan Bank and Nerude Bank in Nepal; Compartamos Banco in Mexico; ACLEDA Bank in Cambodia; BANEX in Nicaragua; JSC Bank Constanta in Georgia; and Erste Bank AD Podgorica in Montenegro (see Table 12). These institutions were all NGOs before they transformed into regulated FIs or directly into a MFB. The same institutions were also selected by several authors who analyse the transformation of MFIs. However, they list all types of MFIs with different forms of legal transitions (Fernando, 2004; Hartarska and Nadolnyak, 2007). Lauer (2008); Campion and White (2001) and Hishigsuren (2006) especially describe NGOs which also changed their legal status into different forms of MFIs, including FIs and MFBs.

The last part of the analysis applies the data of the MFBs in order to describe possible ways forward for the MCAs. Al-Amana, FBPMC and FONDEP are the largest MCAs in Morocco and thus have the potential to transform into regulated MFBs. Their possible development is described in terms of four key areas: *Sustainability, outreach, corporate governance, and regulation*. These issues are mainly discussed in the context of transforming MFIs, e. g. in Mersland and Øystein Strøm (2009, 2008); Hermes *et al.* (2008); Hartarska and Nadolnyak (2007); Quayes (2011), and (Campion and White, 2001) (see Chapter 4.2.2 and also Figure 13).

1 108 banks delivered data to the MIX dataset in 2008 as of 02/2012. In other years, less institutions provided data.

3 Financial Systems and Microfinance Institutions

3.1 The Moroccan financial system and microfinance sector

The Moroccan financial system

The Moroccan financial system is relatively well developed by regional standards. It has many similarities with the French financial system due to their historical connection (Reille and Lyman, 2005; Atallah and El Hyani, 2009). According to the IMF Country Report 2008, the Moroccan *banking sector* is stable, adequately capitalized, and profitable. Banks play a central role in the Moroccan financial sector, as bank assets were equal to 109% of Gross Domestic Product (GDP) in 2007 (IMF, 2008). However, a lot of Moroccan FIs remain concentrated in urban areas, and the government keeps an influence over many banks. There is no Islamic banking in Morocco (Reille and Lyman, 2005; Atallah and El Hyani, 2009). The banking sector comprises 16 banks, 11 of which are private (six majority domestically owned and five majority foreign owned), and five of which are public institutions (two commercial and three specialized banks). As a consequence the government continues to hold 23% of the banking sectors' assets. Six offshore banks share 2% of the financial system assets. Additionally, there are multiple consumer credit financing, mortgage, leasing, factoring, money transfer, and guarantee companies (IMF, 2008). In terms of bank concentration, there are six banks dominating the Moroccan banking sector's assets. The two largest banks have a 51% market share, and four medium-sized banks hold 34% of banking assets. They are mainly composed of loans on the asset side (64% claims on the economy). Banks' liabilities make up 82%, which results in relatively large margins. Thus, Moroccan banks maintain profitability (IMF, 2008; Atallah and El Hyani, 2009).

The Moroccan *NBFIs* hold approximately one third of the country's financial system's assets. Among them is the public *Caisse de Dépot et de Gestion*. With an asset market share of around 5%, it is Morocco's largest NBFI. The institution plays an important role in the primary market, and it is the second largest institution on the secondary market for treasury securities. Furthermore, the *Poste du Maroc* has a key function in providing depository, payments, and other retail banking services for small savers (IMF, 2008). It represents a postal savings system with national coverage. Its broad post office branching structure allows for an outreach even in remote rural areas (Reille and Lyman, 2005). The Moroccan *banking supervision* complies with the majority of the *Basel Core Principles for Effective Banking Supervision*. The banks' minimum capital adequacy ratios are well above the prescribed Basel II ratios. Non-performing loans in overall banks' portfolios have decreased significantly during recent years (from around 11% in 2006 to around 8% in 2007). However, banks still register high levels of non-performing loans, which are mainly concentrated in public banks. In comparison to emerging countries in Europe, the Moroccan banking sector shows adequate levels of capitalization, solvency, and profitability, but at the same time a higher ratio of non-performing loans (IMF, 2008).

As for banking supervision, it is the Moroccan *central bank* Banque Al Maghrib (BAM) that regulates the local banking sector. Most of the supervised institutions do not explicitly target poor people as customers. None of them provide a significant volume of very small loans, mainly because of economic constraints imposed by applicable interest rate caps and related loan price controls. However, all citizens have a legally guaranteed access to current accounts through the BAM if they are refused at other institutions (Reille and Lyman, 2005).

Moreover, the *capital markets* represent a growing share of the financial sector. Stock market capitalization stood at 73% of GDP in 2006 and 98% of GDP in 2007. By contrast, a move by corporates from bank credit toward the capital markets is still limited in scope. The number of traded stocks is also limited (63% in 2006, 73% in 2007). Trades are concentrated in relatively few stocks (six stocks accounted for 71% of trades in 2007). Therefore, banks continue to be the main source of private sector financing, and government securities dominate the non-bank debt market (IMF, 2008).

Concerning the Moroccan *stock market* development, fewer than 50,000 persons hold shares in Morocco. Stock market capitalization grew to around 90% of GDP in 2007 even though trading remains concentrated on a few stocks only. The Casablanca Stock exchange is one of the oldest exchanges on the African continent. In sum, capital markets increasingly contribute to financial deepening (IMF, 2008; Reille and Lyman, 2005).

Morocco's *insurance sector* is relatively small by emerging countries' standards. It is a stable and concentrated market which has grown steadily over the past few years (12% in 2006 and 20% in 2007). 17 insurance and even one re-insurance company, the *Central Reinsurance Company*, share 16% of the financial system assets. The largest three account for 53% of the insurance market. The average insurance premium is less than USD 65 per capita. Furthermore, the insurance institutions are not affiliated with banks. The Moroccan insurance market is the second largest in Africa after South Africa, and it is the leading one in the Arab world citepIMF2008. The access to banking services has already greatly improved over time. The percentage of population holding a bank account increased to 40% in2007 from 15% in 2002, and credit volume doubled since 2001. This is due to increased competition as well as the need to diversify risks following the Basel principles. In addition, the favourable economic environment stimulates the progress. Thus, the number of bank branches has increased by 12% in 2007, and the number of Automated Teller Machines (ATM) has tripled over the past five years (IMF, 2008).

Describing the financial development of the Moroccan financial sector, Bennaceur *et al.* (2011) uses data from the *Financial Development and Structure Database*. This is a database of indicators which measure the size, activity, and efficiency of financial intermediaries and markets (Beck *et al.*, 2010). Tables 1 and 2 show the financial development indicators and banking sector assets from 2005 to 2009. The Moroccan indicators are compared to the MENA region as well as to lower middle income countries and OECD countries (high income countries). Morocco is identified as a lower middle income country according to the World Bank (Beck *et al.*, 2000). It is noticeable that all Moroccan indicators are higher than the average indicators for the MENA region and even for the countries in the same income class. Furthermore, all indicators increase over time, which partly indicates a positive financial development. For example, the first indicator in Table 1 is *Liquid Liabilities over GDP*. According to King and Levine (1993), this ratio is a measure for financial depth. It results from the idea that the size of financial intermediaries is positively related to the provision of financial services. The Moroccan indicators are almost as high as those of the OECD countries. This can be interpreted as a sign for the relatively high degree of financial sector development in Morocco, as mentioned above. The ratio *Financial System Deposits over GDP* is an indicator for the financial resources banks have available to finance their lending activities. The position *Financial System Deposits* also includes banking deposits (Beck *et al.*, 2010). The indicators again show higher values for Morocco than for MENA and low middle income countries. The indicator *Bank Credit to Bank Deposits* is an important measure for the extent to which banks mobilize savings. According to Honohan and Beck (2007), this ratio increases with the level of economic and financial sector development. Thus, a high ratio indicates a high financial intermediation efficiency. However, ratios above 100% indicate that deposits are not the banks' only funding source and loans not their only assets. Thus, private sector lending is also funded by non-deposit sources, which can lead to funding instability (Beck *et al.*, 2010). While as mentioned above the Moroccan indicators are much higher than those of the MENA region, they are almost equal to values assigned to their income class. As stated in Beck *et al.* (2010) high income countries possess ratios above 100%. The last ratio in Table 1, *Stock Market Capitalization over GDP*, is growing over time in Morocco. The indicator growth shows that the capital market contributes increasingly to the financial deepening in Morocco (IMF, 2008).

The banking sector indicators for Morocco, the MENA region, and the lower middle and high income countries are presented in Table 2. According to Bennaceur *et al.* (2011), the specific banking sector indicators of cost and performance are similar across all MENA countries. The values for the first indicator in Table 2, the *Net Interest Margin*, indicate that costs of financial intermediation are similar to OECD countries and are partly lower than in lower middle income countries. The *Bank Concentration* ratio (market share of the three largest banks' assets over the total banking sector assets) indicates a relatively high concentration in Morocco, as mentioned above. High market concentration is often considered to be an indicator of weak competitiveness, but can increase the banks' profits (Nguyen, 2011). The indicators Return on Assets (ROA) and Return on Equity (ROE) show a strong performance for Morocco. The Moroccan bank income ratio has also improved over time, and it is outperforming the compared regional averages. However, there is an increased awareness of financial markets and FI's development after the financial crisis of 2007 (Bennaceur *et al.*, 2011). The financial authorities in the MENA region are also concerned with risks resulting from liberalization programs. They intend to privatize, modernize, and open their banking systems to foreign banks (Bennaceur *et al.*, 2011). Demirgüç-Kunt and Detragiache

(1998) states that banking crises are more likely to occur in liberalized financial systems. Therefore, the authors suggest that financial liberalization should be approached cautiously where the institutions are not fully developed.

Despite this progress, access to bank credit is limited to a small segment of the economy. This includes only larger enterprises and an estimated 10% of the population with a fixed income or property to give as collateral. It is mainly the Moroccan MCAs who give access to financial services to the rest of the population. The penetration rate of banking and microfinance services also remains low in rural areas. Over 75% of bank credits are concentrated in Casablanca and Rabat. Casablanca absorbs 62% of all private sector credit, a figure that has been increasing since 2002. The five major cities in Morocco also account for more than half of all bank branches (IMF, 2008).

The Moroccan microfinance sector

Microfinance services in Morocco were first offered in 1993 (Atallah and El Hyani, 2009). By 1997 five MFIs were present in the sector. One year later the Moroccan government and the United Nations Development Programme (UNDP) launched the *Micro Start program.* Its objective was to improve access to financial services for low income micro-entrepreneurs. The programme was supposed to enable them to develop their professional activities, increase their incomes, and create new jobs. Between 1998 and 2001 the program provided financial and technical assistance to six MFIs. Furthermore, the government provided financial support to the first MCAs through the government fund *Hassan II*, which was created in the year 2000 and granted a EUR 100 million subsidy to the microfinance sector. Thus, both vehicles contributed significantly to the strengthening of microfinance in Morocco (Atallah and El Hyani, 2009).

Today Morocco has the best performing MFIs in the Arab world (Reille, 2010, 2009). However, from 2007 onward the Moroccan microfinance sector had been affected by a financial crisis. This crisis was characterized by falling returns, expending write-off values, and an extreme hike in asset quality costs (Reille, 2010, 2009). Until 2007 the success of the microfinance sector was mainly due to the support of the Moroccan government. The *Microcredit Associations Law of 1999* provided clear regulations and guidelines for the development of the industry (see also Appendix C). The law states that some non-profit associations in Morocco are exclusively licensed by the ministry of finance. They are allowed to provide microcredit services for income-generating activities as well as housing and social loans with a maximum of 50,000 Moroccan Dirham (MAD) (approcimatelt 5,000 Euro). The BAM took over their supervision in 2007, and the ministry of finance ensured close monitoring. In addition, the international donor community supported the MCAs, mainly USAID and the European Commission. Later the funds were relayed by development FIs such as IFC and KfW. Moreover, the microfinance sector had the commitment from local banks. They have been important backers of the industry, funding 85% of the sector's assets in 2008. Furthermore, these commercial banks created two MCAs in Morocco (FBPMC by Banque Populaire and Fondation Crédit Agricole by Crédit Agricole) (Cohen and Goodwin-Groen, 2004; Reille and Lyman, 2005; Reille, 2009, 2010; Atallah and El Hyani, 2009). By the end of 2007 the Moroccan microfinance sector still showed astonishing portfolio growth (see Figure 1). But with the increase of the credit portfolio the amount of non-performing loans also rose significantly from 0.4% in 2003 to 1.9% in 2007. Other portfolio quality indicators such as the PAR>30 days value (5% end of 2008 and 10% by mid 2009) and the total amount of write-off values increased. In May 2009 the former MCA Zakoura reported a PAR>30 of over 30%. Previously, Zakoura had undertaken aggressive growth in order to compete with the MCA Al Amana. Some leading MCAs also diversified their loan products and offered larger loans with poor underwriting policies (Reille, 2009). Therefore, the cause of the microfinance crisis was due to unsustainable growth of the MCAs assets and loan portfolios. The lack of internal controls, obsolete management information systems, substandard governance, and lenient credit policies were boosting the crisis (Reille, 2009). Moreover, changes in credit policies such as the provision of individual loans, increases in loan size, and changes in payment frequencies led to loan delinquency. Multiple lending was a biasing factor as well. Multiple lending or *l'endettement croisé* occurs when clients maintain loans from two to five different FIs. The global financial crisis did not have an effect on the Moroccan microfinance crisis, even though both crisis occurred almost simultaneously (Reille, 2010, 2009; Chen *et al.*, 2010; JAÏDA, 2011).

As a consequence of the microfinance sector crisis, the Moroccan government organized a merger of two of the biggest MCAs: FBPMC and Zakoura. FBPMC was backed by a solid, government owned bank. The Zakoura association suffered from portfolio deterioration that subsequently made a merger unavoidable. As an additional support, development finance institutions kept their claims in both institutions, and the local commercial banks maintained their credit allocations. Furthermore, both MCAs slowed down their growth and reduced their balance sheets. The restructuring of credit processes as well as judicial action against delinquent borrowers were among the measures taken to overcome the microfinance crisis. MCAs also started to exchange credit information in order to avoid multiple lending practices. Moreover, small and medium-size MCAs cut costs and shared resources by merging or sharing back office systems (Reille, 2010, 2009). Equally important was the government's introduction of a plan to consolidate the microfinance sector in collaboration with the BAM and the Fédération Nationale des Associations de Microcrédit (FNAM). The BAM produced a new directive to strengthen the governance of MFIs and improve transparency. Moreover, the Moroccan government secured USD 46 million from the *Millennium Challenge Account*, a development program, to provide capital and technical assistance to MCAs (see also Appendix C). To control multiple lending and prevent over-indebtedness (Reille, 2009) plans exist to integrate the three largest MCAs into one single credit bureau set up by BAM (Reille, 2009). A credit bureau in general aims to mitigate asymmetric information between borrowers and lenders (see also Appendix C) (Luoto *et al.*, 2007). The government has also shown its willingness to secure liquidity for the sector beyond 2009. Funding linkages are encouraged between MCAs and banks. As two MCAs have been established by local banks, smaller MCAs are also being encouraged to find bank sponsors (Reille, 2009).

In December 2010, eight out of twelve MCAs accounted for a total outstanding portfolio of USD 570 million and 807,000 active borrowers.(see Figure 1). Three major MCAs, Al Amana, FONDEP, and FBPMC, dominate the sector, covering around 93% of gross total loan portfolio in the microfinance sector. Equally important, Morocco remains the most advanced microfinance sector in the Arab world in terms of outreach (59% of the total regional customers) and loan volume (around 96% of total Arab funds), as shown in Table 4 (Reille, 2009, 2010). After already showing high growth rates during 2004 and 2005 the Moroccan microfinance sector experienced a veritable boom in the following two years. The aggregate loan portfolio rose from USD 163 million in early 2006 to USD 721 million at the end of 2007, and the number of clients doubled from 627,000 to 1,300,000. With the opening of nearly 900 branches, almost 3,500 new employees were hired in only three years (2005-2007) (Reille, 2010). The growing demand for microcredit loans led to a change in lending policies. Individual loan products gradually supplanted solidarity or group loan products. As part of this development the share of female borrowers also declined from 68% in 2005 to 48% in 2008 (see Figure 1). Female borrowers used to be the main beneficiaries of group loans (Reille and Lyman, 2005). The level of domestic borrowing is relatively high in Morocco compared to other countries in the Arab world. 83% of MFIs' assets are mainly financed by local FIs. Half of that amount comes from commercial banks. In recent years, the main MCAs have become more and more independent from secured financing or grants from donors. Figure 1 shows the change in the MCA's funding structure. Equity investments (subsidies contributed to equity) have declined over time and have changed to debt financing (Atallah and El Hyani, 2009). Even during the Moroccan microfinance crisis commercial banks kept their claims in the MCAs. Normally the MFIs would have experienced a lack of liquidity in their sector because of a slowdown in bank lending since banks are generally averse to grant loans to sectors in crisis. However, that was not the case in Morocco for several reasons:

- the crisis was expected to be temporary;
- MFIs benefiting from bank loans maintained strong relationships with banks; and
- the Moroccan government supported the links between MCAs and commercial banks (Reille and Lyman, 2005; Reille, 2010).

In terms of the loan characteristics from commercial banks, compared to other regional institutions the MCAs benefit from resources with longer maturities and relatively low interest rates. Loans for MCAs have an average loan maturity of 82 months and a weighted average interest rate of 4.77% (see Table 5). There are also differences within the sector. These preferable funds are mostly granted to the main actors Al Amana, FONDEP, and FBPMC. Furthermore, Figure 1 shows a relatively good financial performance of the institutions with a median value of ROA between 4% and 6%. However, the MCAs' profitability has decreased strongly since the sector crisis. It has reached a median value of only 0.2% in 2009 when half of the MFIs reported negative returns. Aside from this the institutions' portfolio quality deteriorated since 2007. Figure 1 shows the declining PAR and write-off values after that date. In addition, financial incomes declined sharply after 2006. Expenses rose accordingly, especially from 2007 until 2009. The level of loan loss provision expenses was relatively stable until 2007 (2% to 3%). Then the rate doubled every year between 2007 and 2009. However, the level of financing costs has remained relatively constant. This shows that the MCAs still had the ability to raise debt (see Figure 1) (Atallah and El Hyani, 2009). The decline in operating expenses in 2009 is mostly due to policies initiated by the MCAs that resulted mostly in branch closures and downsizing of staff (Reille, 2009). According to the FNAM (2012), twelve non-profit associations hold permits to operate as MCAs under the 1999 Microcredit Associations Law (see also Table 3). The institutions registered as associations are effectively the only players in the microcredit market. None of the other available legal forms of MFIs are able to operate sustainable microlending portfolios due to interest rate caps and related loan pricing controls. Since the adoption of the Microcredit Associations Law there are also no more branch operations of foreign NGOs that can carry out lending activities directly. Finally, the MCAs differ in terms of their size, growth, operating markets, as well as their methodology, and product offerings (Reille and Lyman, 2005). Three organizations account for more than 90% of the microfinance gross loan portfolio, over 80% of active borrowers and over 70% of operating offices in Morocco (see also Table 6). These organizations are more concentrated in urban and peri-urban areas, and they are branching rapidly into new product offerings (Atallah and El Hyani, 2009; Reille and Lyman, 2005). The share of urban and rural population in Morocco also supports the target choice as 57% of the population live in cities (see Table 24). However, there might be potential for microfinance clients in the rural area as well. The new product offerings were made possible by a change in the Microcredit Associations Law. Some of the other associations are more similar to the three biggest MCAs in terms of their geographic reach, product offerings, and balance sheet structure. Others in turn have chosen more specific hard-to-serve geographic or sectoral markets. They are pursuing these markets with specially designed products and lending methodologies. The association *Fondation de Crédit Agricole* for example works exclusively with farm families in remote rural areas. There are also associations that remain very small. They show lower performance measures and will probably require significant ongoing donor funds (Atallah and El Hyani, 2009; Reille and Lyman, 2005).

3.2 Profiles of the main Moroccan microcredit associations

Microcredit association Al Amana in Rabat, Morocco

Al Amana was launched in 1997 as an association for Moroccan law and rights. Later, in March 2000, the association received the approval from the ministry of finance to operate as a MCA. In the next two years Al Amana ensured its financial and institutional autonomy by improving their microfinance activities in terms of scale and scope, and it received multiple awards from several prize committees. From 2007 until 2009, Al Amana introduced a concept to allow the *bancarisation de masse*, which is defined as the concentration of banking services in a certain population. Thus, Al Amana has expanded its financial services in order to reach more clients and to allow them to gain access to financial services (Al Amana, 2010).

Today, the mission of Al Amana is to promote microenterprises. The MCA makes credit available to commercial microentrepreneurs and artisans that are currently excluded from the traditional financial system. Al Amana's main funding sources are grants and loans. In return, the institution offers loans, training, consulting, and assistance (MIXMarket, 2010). The Al Amana loan product range includes loans for individuals, enterprises and housing loans. The MCA also takes part in government supported programs just like the *l'Initiative Nationale de Développement Humain* and *Villes Sans Bidonvilles*. The latter can realize housing loans in order to rebuild slum areas. The *Agence Française de Développement* invested 10 million Euros which Al Amana manages to grant loans (Al Amana, 2010). Strategically they focus on extension, diversification of their activities, international development, and institutional transformation into a MFB. Al Amana is currently the leading MCA in Morocco, and it is very active in the institutional transformation process (Atallah and El Hyani, 2009; Allaire *et al.*, 2009). There are several institutions supporting Al Amana, among others: JAIDA and FNAM (see Appendix C), ACCION, CGAP, Women's World Banking, IFC and PlanetFinance, Commercial Banks such as Citibank, Société Générale, Crédit du Maroc, Groupe Caisse d'Epargne, and Government related institutions such as the African Development Bank and the EIB (Al Amana, 2010; L'Économiste, 2005, 2007).

After 1997, Al Amana reached the following benchmarks in six years of operation:

- operational sustainability in 2000;
- financial sustainability in 2002;
- 125 branches, more than 100,000 clients, a portfolio amount of USD 8.1 million by 2003; and
- 400 branches all across Morocco, more than 2,000 employees, and 461,000 clients by 2009 (Cohen and Goodwin-Groen, 2004; Atallah and El Hyani, 2009).

Microcredit association FBPMC in Casablanca, Morocco

The FBPMC was founded in March 2000 by the *Groupe Banque Populaire*. At the same time, the association received the approval from the ministry of finance to operate as a MCA. Today its objective is to distribute microcredits for people creating their own business who otherwise would be excluded from financial services. The MCA retains generated profits in order to finance other microcredit related activities, such as consulting, technical assistance, and training (FBPMC, 2010; Atallah and El Hyani, 2009). FBPMC is one of the examples of strong relationships between NGOs and commercial banks. It obtains strong ongoing support in the form of expertise and loan capital from its founder *Banque Populaire*. However, staffing and office space of the two institutions are separated. The MCA contributes to the economic development and wins clients for the bank (Reille and Lyman, 2005). The FBPMC program includes the following items:

- promotion of microenterprises by modernizing their production tools;
- facilitating their transition from the informal to the formal sector of the economy; and
- *bancarisation* of their financial transactions.

FBPMC supports financing, supervision, training, and monitoring of microentrepreneurs. The associations' branches provide the basic structure of the foundation. Furthermore, it manages credit services and customer care independently (FBPMC, 2010). In the course of the Moroccan microfinance crisis, the Zakoura association suffered extremely from portfolio deterioration. As a consequence, Zakoura was liquidated, and the government organized the merger of FBPMC and Zakoura in May 2009 (Reille, 2009).

Microcredit association FONDEP in Rabat, Morocco

The FONDEP is the third biggest MCA in Morocco and was founded in Rabat in 1996. The MCA finances microprojects generating income and promotes very small enterprises. FONDEP also takes part in the improvement of the living conditions of the poor population. Their target groups are women in rural areas and unemployed young people. Individuals or interdependent groups (group lending) can benefit from the association's services. Their clients can start revenue-generating activities in the sectors of handicraft, agriculture, trade or services. FONDEP obtained the ministry approval to operate as a MCA in the year 2000 (FONDEP, 2011; Atallah and El Hyani, 2009). In January 2011, Mrs. Doris Köhn, Senior Vice President of KfW, and Mr. Zine El Abidine Otmani, Director of FONDEP, signed a partnership contract in Rabat. The agreement includes a refundable loan of EUR 10 million with a duration of eight years and a grace period of two years. It is the first mutual agreement between the German development bank KfW and a MCA in Morocco. The KfW accompanies the Moroccan institution in the development of its activity of financial support to poor people (FONDEP, 2011).

3.3 Profiles of selected transformed microfinance banks

ProCredit bank in El Salvador, San Salvador

PCB El Salvador was a former NGO called AMPES. It was founded in 1988, and seven years later AMPES changed its legal status into that of a regulated financial intermediary named *Financiera Calpiá*. Then, in 2004, the institution transformed into a new MFB (GIZ, 2004). In this context, the chairman of the ProCredit Holding (PCH) defines MFBs as institutions which

- *"[...] are subject to supervision by a banking supervisory authority and required to adhere to banking legislation;*
- *have a clear focus on lending to micro and small enterprises; and*
- *attract local deposits which helps the MFB become less reliant on international credit lines."* (Zeitinger, 2004).

Banco ProCredit El Salvador, as well as the other PCBs, are members of the ProCredit group. It comprises 21 banks in Latin-America, Africa, and Eastern Europe. The ProCredit group can be seen as a corporate group in terms of its organizational structure and business policies. The managers of the banks have the autonomy to run their institutions' daily business independently. However, the overall strategy is developed by the group management in Frankfurt, Germany. Therefore, the image presented to customers, the products on offer and the services the banks provide are uniform (Schmidt, 2010). The PCBs lend not only to microbusinesses but also to small and medium sized enterprises. The transformation of PCB El Salvador was supported by an alliance of international development-oriented investors. Today the PCH is the majority owner of Banco ProCredit El Salvador, holding 99.7% of its shares (PCB El Salvador, 2010; Freytag, 2005) (see Table 18).

ProCredit bank in Santa Cruz, Bolivia

In 1992 the financial NGO *Procrédito* was founded in La Paz, Bolivia. The foundation was supported by the German consulting firm International Project Consult (IPC). In 1995 the NGO transformed itself into a Fondo Financiero Privado (FFP) named Caja Los Andes (CLA). It was the first FI licensed under the new microfinance regulations in Bolivia and distinguished itself from its competitors by pursuing individual lending to urban citizens rather than solidarity group loans. In the past, CLA lent money mostly to manufacturers because it believed that the industry had the greatest effects on employment. Later CLA also granted commercial loans. Near the end of 1995, the institution transformed into a MFB named *Banco Los Andes ProCredit*. This was possible mainly by capital injections of public investors. Today PCB Bolivia is one of the biggest banks in Bolivia in its market sector. During the crisis from 2009 to 2010, the bank was recapitalized by its international holding company while another Bolivian MFB, BANEX, had to be liquidated (CGAP, 2005; Navajas *et al.*, 2000; Bédécarrats *et al.*, 2012) (see also Appendix D). The PCB has been a member of the ProCredit group until today. The PCH is the majority owner of the bank and holds 99.96% of its shares (PCB Bolivia, 2010) (see Table 19).

The parent company ProCredit Holding

In 1998 the development finance consultancy IPC founded the Internationale Micro Investitionen AG (IMI) (Schmidt, 2005, 2010), which was later renamed ProCredit Holding AG. It was the first private institution established to invest in commercially-oriented MFBs worldwide. Its founders were investors such as IFC and KfW (Zeitinger, 2004; Alexander, 2005). The upcoming PCBs had an increasing need for equity capital. The required capital amount could not be covered solely by the IPCs' earnings. It was in this context that the IMI was founded as an association for investments in MFBs (Schmidt, 2010). By June 2003 IMI had made investments in 10 institutions in Eastern Europe, five in the

LAC region, and three in Africa and the Philippines. 12 out of 18 institutions that had been founded since 1998 had profit earnings. This was only possible because of the support of many organizations that provided funds and technical assistance. Moreover, they offered training services in order to support the establishment and development of the new MFBs (Zeitinger, 2004). The PCH is committed to expand access to financial services in transition and developing countries. For that purpose they have built a group of banks that are providers of transparent financial services for very small, small, and medium-sized businesses and also for the general population in their countries of operation (Schmidt, 2010). Furthermore, the PCH guides and supports the development of the PCBs e. g. in the areas of banking operations, human resources, and risk management. Moreover, it provides the banks' senior management and ensures that Basel II risk management principles are implemented on the whole group level (PCB Bolivia, 2010). The PCH shareholders are the Dutch *DOEN Foundation*, the US pension fund *TIAA-CREF*, the US *Omidyar-Tufts Microfinance Fund*, and the Swiss investment fund *responsAbility*, as well as the KfW, IFC, FMO, BIO, and Proparco.

On 2 February 2012 ProCredit received a banking license from the German supervisory authorities. Previously, the PCH had not been subject to banking supervision. ProCredit founded a separate company in Germany which applied to the German Federal Financial Supervisory Authority (Bundesanstalt für Finanzdienstleistungsaufsicht (BaFin)) for a banking licence. Furthermore, the PCH applied to be the superordinate company according to the German Banking Act. It was responsible for maintaining an adequate level of equity for the group. It ensured that all reporting, risk management, and compliance obligations required under German banking regulations were met. After having received the banking license, the German ProCredit Bank is now subject to direct supervision and the ProCredit group is subject to consolidated supervision by the BaFin (PCH, 2010).

4 Analysis and Results

4.1 Analysis before the bank transformation

4.1.1 Comparative analysis

This chapter aims to compare the MCAs and the selected MFBs with regard to their institutional development before they were transformed into banks. Several indicators in six different areas can help identify differences between the analysed institutions: Institutional size, clients, performance, outreach, funding structure, and financial intermediation (see Table 7). According to Armendáriz and Morduch (2010) there are five financial ratios which are commonly used to compare the financial performance and sustainability of MFIs. Four out of the five recommended ratios[1] are:

$$OSS = \frac{Operational\ revenue}{Financial\ expense + loan-loss\ provision\ expense + operating\ expense}$$

$$ROA = \frac{Net\ operating\ income-taxes}{Average\ assets}$$

$$PAR > 30days = \frac{Portfolio\ at\ risk\ (after\ 30\ days)}{Gross\ loan\ portfolio}$$

$$Yield\ on\ gross\ loan\ portfolio = \frac{Cash\ financial\ revenue\ from\ loan\ portfolio}{Average\ gross\ loanportfolio}$$

1 The fifth ratio is the FSS (financial self-sufficiency) which cannot be calculated with the data from the MIX dataset.

The Operational Self-sufficiency (OSS) measures the extent to which the operating revenues of a MFI cover its operating costs. A value of 100% indicates full operational self-sufficiency. A value under 100% shows that the institution relies on outside funding to maintain its current level of operation. However, an institution with a value higher than 100% is able to continue operating at its present scale without requiring additional funding or subsidies. Moreover, ROA measures how well an institution uses its total assets to generate returns. The PAR value summarizes all loans outstanding that have one or more instalments with a certain number of days overdue. The last measure presented above is used to assess revenues. The indicator *yield on gross loan portfolio* measures the average interest rate charged to borrowers by the institution or, more generally, the income from the loan portfolio (Armendáriz and Morduch, 2010; Thapa, 2007). Imai *et al.* (2011); Mersland and Øystein Strøm (2008, 2009); Cull *et al.* (2007) and Ahlin *et al.* (2011) also use these indicators to assess the financial performance of MFIs. Additionally, they included the write-off ratio and ROE as a measure of MFI performance.

The institutional size of MFIs is measured by the value of their assets and the number of employees and branches. Measuring and comparing total assets of these banks makes sense as their core business is to grant loans. The MFB's average share of the loan portfolio over assets is greater than 75% (see Table 34). The funding structure is replicated by equity, deposits and borrowings over assets respectively. The financial intermediation is measured by deposits over gross loan portfolio (see also Chapter 3.1).

Outreach measures are split into different ratios. The *depth of outreach* is defined as the access to credit for poor people. The poorer the borrowers are, the greater the depth of outreach. However, it is difficult to measure the depth of outreach because the information about the level of client poverty is either not collected or not revealed due to privacy matters. Therefore the depth of outreach is measured by the loan balance or loan size per borrower. There is a strong positive correlation between income level and the size of loans: The smaller the size of the loan, the poorer the borrower(Quayes, 2011). Hisako (2009) and Hermes *et al.* (2008) use this indicator to measure the depth of outreach, too (see Table 7). Furthermore, the *breadth of outreach* is measured by the number of people a MFI grants credit to, whereas the *scope of outreach* is defined as the number of types of financial contracts supplied, e. g. loans and savings services, loans to groups, and individuals or contracts with different terms. For example, a loan with a principal of USD 100 and one repayment due in one month is another product in comparison to a loan of USD 200 with instalments due each month for a year. Moreover, the *outreach to women* is described as the number of female borrowers divided by the total number of borrowers (Schreiner, 2002). It is also an indicator of the social orientation of MFIs (Gutierrez-Goiria and Goitisolo Lezama, 2011). Women are still the most deprived group of the society. The hope is that access to microcredit can help change this (Maurya, 2011).

The Morrocan MCAs have the legal status of a NGO. Therefore, before their institutional transformation into a MFB, the institutions are compared with other NGOs. The legal status of the MCAs prevents them to fund their assets with mobilized deposits. Thus, they are no FIs in the sense that they can intermediate between savers and borrowers. They also have a non-profit status. Thus, they retain earnings to fund their operations. In Morocco they are exempted from taxes. The three biggest MCAs are all operationally self-sufficient and have a relatively large outreach.

The compared MFBs are those which were NGOs before their sole institutional transformation into a MFB. Lauer (2008) defines this circumstance as a one-stage transformation. A two-stage transformation usually comprises a first transformation from a NGO into a regulated FI and later into a licensed bank. From the 16 selected MFBs that were NGOs before, ten institutions experienced a one-stage transformation and the other six a two-stage transformation. Four out of ten institutions partially provided data before their transformation: Nirdhan Bank and Nerude Bank in Nepal, ADOPEM in the Dominican

Republic, and D-Miro in Ecuador. All institutions are either from the LAC region or the Eastern Europe and Central Asia (EECA) region. The indicators for this comparison are assets, number of active borrowers and employees, average loan balance per borrower, the percentage of female borrowers, OSS, ROA and PAR>30 days (see Table 7). The data of the institutions ranges over the last three years before their transformation. The former NGOs thereby provided data in a time period from 1996 until 2010. The values of D-Miro and the MCAs range from 2008 until 2010. Here, it is important to see how the values, e. g., number of borrowers develop over a three-year period before the transformation and how their mean values differ (see Tables 8 and 9).

The comparison shows that former NGOs had no deposits to finance their loan activity like the MCAs did. Moreover, the NGOs' values of assets were very different from that of the institutions. The smallest MCA has been more than five times bigger than the biggest NGO in this comparative analysis. Compared to the asset values of the transformed MFBs after their transformation, only Banco Compartamos was bigger than the biggest MCA (see Tables 10 and 11). Therefore, even smaller NGOs than the MCAs were able to transform into MFBs. This is one reason why the asset growth rates of the smallest NGOs were much higher than those from the MCAs. The MCAs' stagnating or even declining assets could still be the impact of the Moroccan microfinance sector crisis. The numbers of employees and active borrowers show similar developments. The MCAs reduced costs while NGOs have grown in terms of staff and number of active borrowers, except for D-Miro. However, the absolute number of MCA-employees was higher than that of the NGOs. Increasing the loan balance of the MCAs implies a reduced number of poorer borrowers. The loan balances of D-Miro and Nerdude Bank were also increasing. D-Miro had almost as high an average loan balance as the MCAs. Loan balance growth often leads to reduced costs per borrower and therefore to a higher financial performance. Quayes (2011) and Hermes *et al.* (2008) found that MFIs in general are less efficient if they have a lower average loan balance. Moreover, the percentage of the MCAs' female borrowers waspartly decreasing. The declining number of female borrowers was mainly due to the change of group loans into individual loans (see also Chapter 3.1). Additionally, higher loan balances indicate that the level of social commitment or outreach is lower. The lower amounts primarily relate to women, who generally have lower incomes (Gutierrez-Goiria and Goitisolo Lezama, 2011). The Nepali NGOs maintained their ratios of 100%,reflecting their strategy to provide financial services mainly to poor women (Sharma, 2004; M-Cril, 2008). D-Miro even increased its share of female borrowers. What the MIX data does not show is the development of outreach. However, the loan portfolio of FBPMC has shown a wide range of loan characteristics in terms of the principal size as well as the maturity and frequency of instalments (see Table 29). The loan portfolio characteristics of FBPMC indicate that they have had a great share of group loans. Mersland and Øystein Strøm (2009) found that outreach is greater in the case of group lending than in the case of lending to individuals. For comparison, the different terms of loans and deposits for the PCBs have also been diverse (see Tables 29, 28, 27, 26, 25). Hence, FBPMC already has a wide scope of outreach, despite its NGO status.

Banco ADOPEM and the MCAs were self-sufficient in terms of operation, whereas Nirdhan Bank, Nerude Bank, and D-Miro were not. However, D-Miro had an OSS value of over 100% before 2009. It may have declined due to the international financial crisis. The MCAs have been able to cover their costs in contrast to other NGOs before their bank transformation. The MCAs' OSS values experienced only small changes in the last three years, as was the case for the Nirdhan NGO. The ROA for Al Amana, D-Miro, and Nerude Bank seemed to shrink a lot. However, their mean ROA was also relatively low. In terms of financial performance, FONDEP and FBPMC appeared to recover faster than their competitor Al Amana. Additionally, PAR values of Al-Amana have been higher than those of the other two MCAs. This can be due to changes in loan policies, regulation or raising competition in the microfinance markets. D-Miro and Nerude Bank also had high growth rates regarding the PAR>30 days values.

In conclusion, the analysed values for the institutions are not really similar. There are also differences between the MCAs. This can be due to the low sample of compared institutions. It is notable to see that the MCAs are more developed in terms of institutional size and financial performance than the NGOs. In turn, the Nepali institutions were stronger in terms of outreach. Thus, the MCAs already show typical characteristics of sustainable MFBs. This supports the research of Mersland and Øystein Strøm (2009, 2008) where NGOs already performed as well as regulated shareholder-owned firms.

4.1.2 Discussion about transforming microfinance institutions

In former times MFIs were expected to become independent of donor subsidies (Quayes, 2011). They would achieve financial self-sufficiency as they show high rates of loan recovery (Quayes, 2011). In contrast, Morduch (1999) demonstrates that despite the high recovery rate, donor-dependent MFIs are not able to automatically transform into independent self-sustaining institutions. The concept of institutional transformation was born over a decade ago with the aim to reach two major goals: The first goal was to increase the number of clients with access to microfinance, the second to reduce donor dependencies. This has driven the industry toward greater integration with the formal financial sector, leading a large number of NGOs to consider transformation into privately owned and regulated entities (Campion and White, 2001; Hishigsuren, 2006). As increased efficiency can lead to a trade-off with the MFIs' outreach. In this heated discussion two major parties hold different positions: the *welfarists view* and the *institutionalists view*. The *welfarist view* propagates the dominance of the outreach goal (Montgomery and Weiss, 2005; Hashemi and Rosenberg, 2006; Woller, 2002), whereas the *institutionalists* stress the importance of sustainability and efficiency (Rhyne, 1998; Christen, 2001; Isern and Porteous, 2005). With the recent transformation development in the microfinance sector, a lot of MFIs agree voluntarily to operate as regulated institutions, especially in Latin-America. After the transformation they are for-profit financial institutions that are allowed to collect deposits. Christen (2000) states that 53% of the MFIs in Latin-America are classified as for-profit institutions. An extreme example for microfinance commercialisation is the Initial Public Offering (IPO) of Banco Compartamos in 2007. Its IPO was 13 times oversubscribed. However, since the foundation of the Compartamos NGO in 1990 the institution was funded by grants from different donor agencies (Rosenberg, 2007). In addition, the Compartamos bank does not finance its assets through deposits from the public or loans from development institutions (see Figure 4). Instead the bank funds itself with retained earnings, loans from other banks, and the issuance of bonds on the capital markets (Schmidt, 2010). Furthermore, Cull *et al.* (2009) state that 57% of the analysed sample of 315 international MFIs are profitable firms. Even 54% of 154 NGOs are also for-profit institutions. They serve 87% of 16.1 million borrowers. These numbers are proof that the microfinance industry is normally a profitable one. Additionally, the MIX data show very similar findings. In 2010, 40% of 1101 MFIs were profitable, and they served 57% of almost 60 million borrowers (see Table 16). Ten years earlier, however, only 39% of more than 4 million borrowers were served by for-profit institutions. Despite this, 39% out of 199 MFIs were profitable in the year 2000 (see Table 17). Additional results from this master's thesis and the data provided by the MIXMarket organization also show an increasing number of international MFIs transforming exclusively into MFBs over time (see Figure 12 and Tables 14 and 15).

Reasons for an institutional transformation can be found in several studies, e. g. in Atallah and El Hyani (2009); Armendáriz and Morduch (2010); Olsen (2010). According to Atallah and El Hyani (2009); Lauer (2008); Montgomery and Weiss (2005); Campion and White (2001); Fernando (2004); Armendáriz

and Morduch (2010); Olsen (2010), there are several possible advantages and disadvantages that can apply to Moroccan MCAs.
Advantages can be:

- having access to international financial markets;
- offering deposits and other savings products to the public;
- becoming less reliant on borrowings and/or receiving donations;
- extending the number of clients served;
- offering new financial products and services;
- gaining legitimacy;
- enabling employees, clients, and other stakeholders to become owners;
- complying with new legislation requiring or permitting transformation; and
- improved corporate governance.

Disadvantages can be:

- the Microcredit Association Law is still not modified;
- fear that social aspects will be undermined;
- complying with regulation (rules governing their operations, interest rate limits, foreign ownership limitations, tax and accounting issues); and
- high cost of regulation compliance.

There is no universally valid answer to the question whether a NGO should transform itself into a regulated institution or not. Comparing the advantages and disadvantages of a transformation, the advantages seem to be predominant. Vanroose (2007) also states that a transformation can be advantageous. However, whether or not this reduces poverty is still questionable. Maintaining a social mission can be a too ambitious goal for the transformed institutions. Morduch (2000) doubts that sound MFBs which are able to cover their costs will ensure depth of outreach and the alleviation of poverty. Hence, what is obvious here is that each issue of advantages and disadvantages should be considered and discussed in the framework of the specific MFI characteristics. For instance, for a MCA whose intention it is to offer deposits to the public, have access to international funding sources, and offer new products and services (Atallah and El Hyani, 2009) a transformation seems to be the best option.

4.2 Analysis after the bank transformation

4.2.1 Comparative analysis

This chapter aims to compare the selected MFBs with regard to their institutional characteristics (see indicators in Table 7). The data is structured into two clusters of MFBs . The first cluster contains two PCBs which belong to a group of banks, and their strategy is developed and enforced by the PCH in Germany. The second cluster includes 16 banks which operate independently and as single banking institutions. The goal is to show that different MFBs experienced similar institutional developments. If the institutions' experiences are comparable, the data can be used to describe the possible development of the Moroccan MCAs. The 16 MFBs were selected from a total amount of 106 banks registered in the MIX dataset (see also Chapter 2). According to the MIX dataset and the banks' descriptions on MIXMarket (2010), these 16 banks had been NGOs before their legal status transition (see Table 12). All data is from the MIX dataset in order to make an easier comparison to the second cluster of banks, where the data is also extracted from the MIX dataset.

As a first step, the comparative analysis describes the institutional similarities between the two PCBs and the second cluster of 16 MFBs. This is also important as the data from the PCBs is more detailed than those from the MIX dataset. The second step in this analysis focuses on the development of the institutions and the reasons why some indicators rise or fall.

To begin the analysis, table 12 represents the institutional development of the selected MFBs. The 16 banks are from Latin-America (10 banks), EECA (five banks) and Africa (one bank). Most of the banks are from the LAC region (see Table 13). The NGOs in these countries already experienced their institutional transformation in the 1990s and later until 2009, like other banks in Asia and Africa. It is important to note that the PCBs and ten of the selected MFBs show a so called two-stage transformation (Lauer, 2008), while one case, that of ACLEDA, even experienced a three-stage transformation (see Page D). This comparative analysis includes all indicators mentioned above (see Table 7). The data of the 16 MFBs is displayed over five years and across 16 different indicators relating to the banks' assets. Further descriptions of the indicators are to be found in the MIX Market Glossary in Appendix E). For each indicator the weighted average is calculated for any year in the time period from 2005 until 2010. The starting year 2005 is chosen as it was the date of the PCB transformation in Bolivia. Only data after the transformation of the MFBs is used for the comparison. Then, a corridor is defined around the mean value by adding one standard deviation and vice versa. For instance, if the *equity over assets* value of PCB Bolivia in 2005 is located in-between the corridor of the other MFBs' ratios, the PCB Bolivia might be similar to other transformed MFBs in terms of their *equity over assets* ratio.

The results show that most of the PCBs' values lie in the predefined range of the other banks' values. There are only 13 deviations out of 168 values for the PCBs (see Figures 8, 11, 9, 10). This method was used since the MIX dataset of the MFBs is not complete and because the transformation dates of the banks are different. However, the comparison assumes that the banks have comparable values independently of their operating experience. This is in fact not the case as all of the MFBs' mean values rather differ (see Tables 10 and 11). Furthermore, most of the banks in the second cluster are from the LAC region (10 out of 16). That can have an impact on the results as the PCBs are also located in Latin-America. Moreover, the sample of 16 banks might be too small in order to identify the comparison results as stable. But by March 2012 these were the only transformed institutions to provide data to the already largest public microfinance database worldwide. Finally, using standard deviations in this calculation assumes that the different values per year are normally distributed. The Jarque-Bera test (JB) shall indicate how many variables are normally distributed. Therefore, the chi-square distribution table[2] aims to detect the critical value which defines if the null hypothesis is rejected or not (Brys *et al.*, 2004; Bera and Jarque, 1980). For this normality test, the following null and alternative hypothesis apply:

H_0 : The data is sampled from a normal distribution.
H_1 : The data is not sampled from a normal distribution.

The applicable formulas according to the Jarque-Bera test are:

$$JB = \frac{n}{6}(S^2 + \frac{(K-3)^2}{4}) \tag{4.1}$$

whereas

$$S = \frac{\hat{\mu}_3}{\sigma^3} = \frac{\frac{1}{n}\sum_{i=1}^{n}(\chi_i - \bar{\chi})^3}{(\frac{1}{n}\sum_{i=1}^{n}(\chi - \bar{\chi})^2)^{\frac{3}{2}}} \tag{4.2}$$

$$K = \frac{\hat{\mu}_4}{\sigma^4} = \frac{\frac{1}{n}\sum_{i=1}^{n}(\chi_i - \bar{\chi})^4}{(\frac{1}{n}\sum_{i=1}^{n}(\chi - \bar{\chi})^2)^2} \tag{4.3}$$

The Jarque Bera test finds strong evidence for the assumption of normal distribution at the 5% significance level. This analysis implies that the standard deviation in forming the corridor can be applied and that PCBs are similar to

2 A Chi-Square distribution table can be accessed e. g. on http://people.richland.edu/james/lecture/m170/tbl-chi.html

other transformed banks in the world.

To conclude, this part of the analysis implies that the PCBs are similar to other transformed banks in the world. There are some limitations using this method such as the small sample size and the incomplete data. However, many arguments confirm the similarity of the two clusters, i.e. the low number of deviations for the PCBs compared to the 16 MFBs and the positive results for the normality test.

The following figures compare the institutional development of the PCBs and the other 16 MFBs. The two PCBs show similar developments in terms of their asset growth, staff development, and changes in their loan balance size (see Figure 2). The PCBs' assets rose from 2005 to 2010. However, this growth decreased in 2008 and 2009, mainly due to the impact of the international financial downturn. Other banks' loan portfolios also showed impacts of the financial crisis, as was the case for Banco ADOPEM, ACLEDA Bank, and Compartamos Bank. MiBanco experienced an increasing growth rate of its assets shortly after its bank transformation, too. Due to the increasing demand for loans, these banks' loan portfolio grew in 2004, as did those of the PCBs. In 2008 MiBanco was also affected by the financial crisis in a way which caused its asset growth to shrink until 2010. K-Rep Bank has shown negative growth rates after 2008, too. Moreover, the asset growth of the Nirdhan Bank was affected by the Nepali financial crisis in the year 2000 (Khanal, 2007). However, all banks could increase their total assets and have grown as transformed MFBs (see Figure 7).

The PCBs' loan balance of the disbursed loans have grown since the banking transformation. Especially strong growth rates appeared after the financial crisis in 2008. The increasing loan balance was a strategic decision of the PCH. They therefore stopped disbursing microloans like most microfinance NGOs do. The institutions concentrated more on the financing of small and medium-sized enterprises. When a bank disburses loans with higher balances, it can become more efficient since the disbursement of smaller loans creates higher costs (Hermes *et al.*, 2008). Furthermore, microfinance came under massive criticism because of its potential poverty alleviation as well as the alleged exploitation of poor customers for profit motives (Dichter, 2007; Schicks, 2010). The PCH distanced its banks from these developments, which is why the banks started lending much higher amounts. In addition, the loan balances of the other MFBs were also growing over time (see Figure 5). The banks thus also discovered that higher loan balances lead to less costs and higher efficiency of bank operations.

In contrast, the PCBs' personell growth declined over the years even though the absolute number had been growing since the bank transformation. The reasons for this were the declining asset growth rates and the increasing efficiency of the banks. At the time of the banks' transformation in 2004 and 2005, there was a high demand for loans which caused a high hiring rate. The banks concentrated on their institutional growth and less on cost efficiency as their earnings covered all their expenses. Due to the crisis starting in 2008 the demand for loans decreased, and net income decreased as well. Therefore, less employees were needed. Processes were also optimized, such as the avoidance of redundant job positions and the reduction of fixed costs. The number of staff of other banks rose, too (see Figure 3). This could have been due to the consequence of rising assets.

However, the two selected PCBs have not been similar in terms of their portfolio quality (see Figure 2). PCB El Salvador has been much smaller than PCB Bolivia in institutional size and assets. Although both banks have been operating for a long time, PCB Bolivia has operated more branches and therefore has had a higher client proximity. Furthermore, PCB Bolivia has been one of the biggest MFBs in Bolivia in terms of assets and deposits (see Table 14) (ASFI, 2011; Bédécarrats *et al.*, 2012), and El Salvador was much more affected by the financial crisis than Bolivia in terms of GDP growth rate (CEPAL, 2011). Their write-off ratio has risen since the crisis in 2009. Additionally, the Par >30 days has increased since 2010. There will probably be higher PAR values in 2012 as they have lent money to clients from a certain branch. Some of their clients may default in the near future. Furthermore, PCB El Salvador has had more difficulties to recover their debt as crime rates and gang problems are much higher in El Salvador than in Bolivia (World Bank, 2011; Seelke, 2011; The Economist, 2011).

The funding side of the two institutions also shows similarities (see Figure 2). The banks followed a strategy according to which they needed to fund themselves sufficiently with deposits in order to be less dependent on loans from FIs. This is one of the reasons why deposits rose over assets after the bank transformation, and other funding ratios declined. Moreover, a lot of clients used the opportunity to pay their money into a deposit account instead of holding cash amounts. According to the indicators in the *New Database on Financial Development and Structure*, total bank deposits rose in Bolivia and El Salvador (see Tables 32 and 33). MiBanco, Banco ADEMI, BancoSol, ACLEDA and K-Rep Bank show similar funding structures as the PCBs in Bolivia and El Salvador as the share of deposits was rising over time and other funding shares declined (see Figure 4).

4.2.2 Discussion about the possible way forward for the microcredit associations

There are four different, broad issuesmainly discussed in the literature concerning MFI transformation: Outreach, sustainability, corporate governance, and regulation (see also Chapter 2). The following analysis concentrates on these issues addressing possible development opportunities of the MCAs. There are studies which analyse the subjects in connection with sustainability, e. g. in Mersland and Øystein Strøm (2009, 2008); Hermes *et al.* (2008) and Hartarska and Nadolnyak (2007). They show that neither outreach, governance or regulation have an effect on sustainability of transformed institutions (Mersland and Øystein Strøm, 2009, 2008; Hermes *et al.*, 2008; Hartarska and Nadolnyak,

2007). However, other research confirmed that increased sustainability has a positive effect on outreach (Quayes, 2011) and governance (Campion and White, 2001).

Outreach

Schreiner (2002) argues that *financial sustainability* and *depth of outreach* are two desirable but opposite targets. Depth of outreach implies an increased number of poor households which are served by the MFIs. In contrast, financial sustainability can cut the disbursement of smaller loans to poor households or force the MFIs to rely more on subsidies. Schreiner (2002) criticises the one-dimensional analysis on depth of outreach. He demonstrates that other measures like the breadth and scope of outreach can compensate for a lack of depth (Schreiner, 2002).

The results of this study show that all MFBs disburse higher loan balances after their transformation, which in turn means a decreased depth of outreach (see Figures 5 and 2). The banks may serve fewer poor people, who are able to cope with higher loan sizes. This is a typical phenomenon for MFIs that intend to operate in a profitable way. Cull *et al.* (2007) show that MFIs are able to maintain profitability and depth of outreach as long as they avoid granting loans to the absolute poor. Moreover, Navajas *et al.* (2000) demonstrates that most of MFI clients are the richest among the poor population of a region or country. The PCBs also apply the strategy to support small- and medium-sized enterprises and to step out of the often saturated original microfinance markets. In contrast, the breadth of outreach increases for all analysed institutions as the number of borrowers and depositors has increased after the institutions' transformation (see Figure 5). This is mainly due to the improved access to funding sources and the possibility to collect deposits from the public (Campion and White, 2001). The scope of outreach is also wide for the analysed MFBs. All MFBs offer savings services besides loans, except for Banco Compartamos. Furthermore, they all offer different loan products (see

Page D). The different PCB terms of loans and deposits for are shown in Tables 25, 26, 27, 28, and 30. Finally, the outreach to female borrowers is relatively stable. The banks maintain their ratio of female borrowers (see Figure 5).

In conclusion, while the depth of outreach decreases, the outreach to female borrowers does not change, and the breath and scope of outreach is increasing with the legal status transition. The results show a possible trade-off between depth of outreach and sustainability. However, if other forms of outreach increase or remain stable, the trade-off cannot hold for all forms of outreach. Manos and Yaron (2009) state that a trade-off between sustainability and outreach can exist in the short-term. But both can be improved in the long-term. This is possible through an increasing economy of scale and the utilization of improved operational innovations. Additionally, the analysed MFBs are operating over several years, and this can be the reason for the positive outreach values.

Sustainability

The increased focus within the microfinance industry on financial sustainability and efficiency is due to a number of developments:

- increasing competition among MFIs;
- technological change that has also become available for MFIs; and
- financial liberalization and regulation policies (Rhyne and Otero, 2006).

These developments have encouraged MFIs to change their behaviour and broaden their services and activities (Hermes *et al.*, 2008; Karlan and Zinman, 2008). The increased competition for MFIs can lead to e. g. lower interest rates, lower costs, more efficiency, and the introduction of new financial products and services like saving accounts and insurance services. Since the late 1990s, Bolivia has experienced increasing competition in the microfinance industry (Rhyne and Otero, 2006). Interest rates decreased from 30% in 1998 to 21% in 2005. Moreover, Bolivian MFIs have become more efficient. They have also increased the range of financial services which they offer to their clients (Rhyne and Otero, 2006). Furthermore, more advanced banking technology like charge cards, ATMs, the use of cell phones and the internet have helped to reduce costs and improve the delivery of services (Hartarska and Nadolnyak, 2007; Rhyne and Otero, 2006; Kapoor *et al.*, 2007). Finally, several developing countries have recently liberalized financial markets (Hartarska and Nadolnyak, 2007). At the same time, they have implemented regulations to improve the stability of the microfinance industry. These changed financial market policies contribute to improve the sustainability and efficiency of MFIs (Hartarska and Nadolnyak, 2007).

All MFBs show relative equal OSS values, if financial performance is measured by the indicators described by Armendáriz and Morduch (2010). They typically sustain a range between 100% and 140%. In addition, their ROA values range roughly between 1% until 5%, except for Banco Compartamos and ADOPEM, which show higher values. However, ROA values are decreasing slightly. The same results can be seen for the PAR>30 days values. They stand between 0.5% and 4% (see Figure 6). However, BancoSol has significantly decreasing PAR values, and ACLEDA bank has the lowest constant values. PCB El Salvador shows increasing values after 2008 (see Chapter 4.2.1). Finally, the yields on loan portfolios, adjusted for inflation rates, are between 10% and 30% for most of the MFBs. Again, Banco Compartamos and ADOPEM have higher yields. However, all banks show a decline in their yield values in 2008 as a sign of the international financial crisis. Half of the institutions which are analysed here had once been NGOs. The others were already regulated FIs. Mersland and Øystein Strøm (2008) and Mersland and Øystein Strøm (2009) state that being a shareholder-owned and regulated firm does not improve MFI performance. In other words, there are no differences in profitability between NGOs and shareholder-owned firms. However, Banco ADOPEM and Bancamia have increased their OSS, ROA, and yields on their loan portfolio shortly after their bank transformation. Karlan and Zinman (2008) states that some MFIs achieve self-sufficiency by increasing interest rates, which is here the rising yield on gross loan portfolio.

Corporate Governance

Generally speaking NGOs have no owners and are often capitalized with the help of grants (Campion and White, 2001; Fernando, 2004). With their institutional transformation, the MFIs' capital base changes from donated equity and retained earnings to share capital. They create an ownership structure of individuals or legal entities which seek for returns in some form. The transformation of NGOs into regulated FIs generally attracts a small amount of private sector ownership (Campion and White, 2001; Fernando, 2004). The MFIs analysed in the study of Campion and White (2001) involve some private investors, bothindividual and corporate, as well as employees and in some cases also the members of the NGO (e. g., CARD NGO, Philippines). The board of such a transformed institution is usually formed by representatives of the new shareholders (see Table 22). However, public development agencies, the founder NGOs, and specialized funds are the largest investors in most transformed MFIs (see shareholder structures of different institutions in Tables 18, 19, 20, 21, and 23). There are also specialized equity funds, e. g. ProFund, the ACCION Gateway Fund, and IMI. ProFund was the first microfinance investment fund worldwide. In 2011, the first microfinance fund in Germany was created by the Invest in Visions company (Reille *et al.*, 2011; Reinert, 2011). Specialized equity funds, e. g. ACCION and IMI, are no purely private investors. They are important actors in the transformation process towards increased commercial investment in microfinance (Campion and White, 2001; Fernando, 2004). These organizations have also played key roles e. g. in technical assistance (see Chapter 3.3 and Appendix D). Fernando (2004) argues that this form of ownership structure is important because some institutions fear the dominance of private capital. The latter can dilute the social mission of the MFIs. Instead, private investors may direct the NGOs' operations away from its original target groups. Thus, the NGOs are looking for investors whose interest is guided by the so called *double bottom line* (Dieckmann, 2007). The double bottom line allows banks on the one hand to show their corporate social responsibility; but on the other hand these investments provide attractive risk-return profiles. Social investors can be commercial banks such as Citigroup, Deutsche Bank, and HSBC, which all have separate microfinance divisions (Dieckmann, 2007; de Sousa-Shields, 2006). Despite the capital investments in transforming NGOs, the ownership structure of MFBs, particularly Latin-America and Asia, does not differ a lot after their transformation. There are also founder NGOs which maintain a meaningful capital share in the transformed institutions, e. g. ACLEDA and Banco ADOPEM. Exceptions are those banks which increased their share of equity significantly, like in the case of Banco Compartamos (see also Chapter 4.1.2). Fernando (2004) states that transformation brings improvements in governance. The transformation enables the broader participation of international expertise in the board of directors. This is especially visible for some cases in Latin-American, where a liberal environment for foreign equity participation dominates. ACLEDA Bank and K-Rep bank especially benefit from the attendance of international experts on their board of directors.

There are several studies discussing the effect of ownership and sustainability on transformed MFIs. In contrast to Fernando (2004), Mersland and Øystein Strøm (2008) demonstrates that the difference between shareholder owned MFIs and NGOs in terms of the firm performance is minimal. These results are not necessarily surprising since the studies from the general banking markets support their findings. Mersland and Øystein Strøm (2009) shows that financial performance improves with local rather than international directors. They also argue that an internal board auditor and a female CEO will also enhance financial performance. Finally, Alexander (2005) states that the key success factors of the PCBs are ownership, sound governance and good management.

Regulation

Different authors discuss the possibilities for the development of MCAs in terms of regulations, e. g. Reille and Lyman (2005) and Atallah and El Hyani (2009). Reille and Lyman (2005) directly proposes the introduction of amendments of the Microcredit Association Law to permit the transformation of MCAs. The most important barrier to the institutional transformation of top-performing associations can be the interest rate caps they would face as licensed credit institutions. The interest caps make it unprofitable for banks and other credit institutions to grant loans directly. Instead of interest rate capsReille and Lyman (2005) suggests a period of experimentation during which alternative strategies would be tested. Alternative strategies can be stringent transparent loan cost disclosure requirements or financial literacy training for clients. In addition, the IMF (2008) report criticizes the current regulation of MCAs. The authors recommend an appropriate form of prudential supervision if MCAs should be authorized to take retail deposits from the general public (IMF, 2008). Under many countries' laws there is not a completely clear legal path for a microfinance NGO to form a commercial institution. A NGO would transform into a regulated institution by exchanging its portfolio and other property in return for shares in the new company. The Microcredit Associations Law can be interpreted as a permission to a basic exchange transaction that represents such a transformation (Reille and Lyman, 2005). However, the law prohibits a MCA to exist for any purpose other than disbursing microcredits. Furthermore, the MCAs are not explicitly prohibited from becoming shareholders of a bank or any other FI. Nonetheless, the BAM can refuse an application for a license with an association as a substantial shareholder. Possible difficulties can occur in the association's fiscal and also perhaps practical capacity to respond to a capital call (Reille and Lyman, 2005).

Therefore, Atallah and El Hyani (2009) propose three perspectives for the MCAs:

- transformation into a FI (without public deposits) or into a specialized MFB;
- modification of the Microcredit Associations Law by allowing for more activities and other legal forms of MFIs; or
- extension of the Microcredit Associations Law by allowing more financial and non-financial activities as well as improved access to international funding sources.

According to information provided by Al Amana, the Microcredit Association Law may be modified in the near future.

Other microfinance regulatory frameworks have proven to be very helpful in some countries, e. g. in Uganda, Indonesia, Peru, and Bolivia. However, this trend is under threat in some places. Governments might fall back on the implementation of interest rate caps. Furthermore, politicians increasingly see microfinance as an attractive target of their attention (Rhyne and Otero, 2006). Olsen (2010) shows evidence that MFIs operating in countries with a supportive regulatory regime will attract more borrowers. His opinion is that such a supportive regime would allow the institutions to accept deposits and to grant loans with interest rate caps. Until today MCAs have not been able to collect deposits, nor do they yet face interest rate caps. Some researchers argue that such regulations can actually hurt the consumer because they inhibit the ability of MFIs to sustain themselves. Others suggest that interest rate caps decrease the transparency of lending organizations. As a result, the institutions can charge fees or other service costs in order to cover the lending expenses of small loans to the poor population. Rhyne and Otero (2006) state that *"[...] most MFIs in our region operate within unclear and often conflicting legislation that does not support the principles of best practices and hinders MFIs from prospering, growing or even transforming into regulated financial institutions."* (Ahmed El-Ashmawi, Sanabel Network, MENA Region). Other regulation frameworks seem to be more advanced. A member from the XAC Bank stated that *[...] the Mongolian environment is friendly, stable and developing. There are no interest rate caps, no restrictions on currency conversion or on repatriation of dividends."* (Ganhuyag Chuluun, XACBank, Mongolia), and *"[...] the regulatory framework is helping our region, especially in Bolivia, Peru an Colombia, where the regulators have understood microfinance."* (Rafael Llosa, Mibanco, Peru) (Rhyne and Otero, 2006).

A country comparison can give a broader view in terms of other regulatory factors which are indirectly affecting the MCAs. The study of Olsen (2010) assesses the role of increased competition in connection with the MFIs' ability to attract borrowers. Addressing this issue, the analysis shows that Bolivia has the highest density of MFIs compared to El Salvador and Morocco (see Table 24). Bolivia is an illustration of competitive microfinance. For a decade the sector has experienced high competition between MFIs, which has resulted in decreasing interest rates. Offering lower prices, Bolivian MFIs have faced enormous pressure to become much more efficient and to broaden their product range by including larger loans (Rhyne and Otero, 2006). Resulting from the relatively low number of MFIs in Morocco, the number of borrowers per MFI might also be greater than in the Latin-American MFIs. Aubert and Sadoulet (2009); Montgomery and Weiss (2005) and Hisako (2009) also state that MFIs which lend to the very poor have had to decrease their depth of outreach. Instead, they have had to increase their share of large loans as competition has grown stronger with the market entry of profit-oriented MFIs. A study of McKim and Hughart (2005) shows that 70% of the analysed MFIs have reduced loans to their primary target group which comprised the poorer people of the population. Furthermore, Olsen (2010) shows that those economies which are more developed can exhibit a more inclusive financial sector. They therefore have a lower demand for microfinance. Thus, countries that are sufficiently developed will not generate as much demand for microfinance as those that have less developed financial sectors. Moreover, Ahlin *et al.* (2011) and Imai *et al.* (2011) present an evidence for complementarity between overall economic performance and MFI performance. Economic growth appears to improve MFI financial performance, and breaking even can be easier to achieve in richer countries. Morocco is indeed a country with a lower middle income and with a current GDP growth rate of 3.7%. MFIs in financially deeper economies also have lower default and operating costs, and they charge lower interest rates, suggesting that financial competition benefits microfinance clients (Ahlin *et al.*, 2011). The Moroccan financial sector is relatively far developed whereas it is also highly concentrated and regulated (see Chapter 3.1).

Olsen (2010) describes the role of international involvement, stating that it has a positive effect on the number of borrowers at each MFI. Therefore, international investors in microfinance can help MFIs reach more people. However, some areas become over-saturated with increased foreign investment (Dieckmann, 2007, 2008). Until now this has not been the case in Morocco where investors are more local than international (see Chapter 3.1). It can thus be advantageous for investors to invest money in future transformed MCAs. However, Wagner (2011) demonstrates that microfinance markets with strong capital inflows, high credit growth rates and rising competition have experienced a substantial decrease in credit growth and deterioration of portfolio quality since 2008. The same developments have occurred in banking sectors in developed countries. Therefore, when microfinance becomes a part of the global financial system, it also loses its resilience towards crisis in domestic and global financial markets (Wagner, 2011). Gonzalez (2007); Krauss and Walter (2008), and Caldéron (2006) proof that microfinance portfolios have a high resilience to economic shocks and seem to be detached from global capital markets.

Crime rates can have an impact on microfinance activities, especially the loan recuperation, as mentioned above for the PCBs (see Chapter 4.2.1 and

Table 24). The analysis supports the statements above that crime rates in El Salvador are higher than in Bolivia. Compared to Morocco, indicators for corruption, organized crime, and homicide are lower. However, the assault rate is much higher in Morocco than in the other two countries (Harrendorf *et al.*, 2010). Addressing the subject of corruption, Ahlin *et al.* (2011) states that MFIs increase their number of clients more slowly where there is more corruption. Consequently, higher corruption may also hinder microenterprises' ability to operate and grow (Ahlin *et al.*, 2011; Fisman and Svensson, 2007). Therefore, lower corruption is positively related to faster extensive MFI growth. Beck *et al.* (2006) also provide an empirical assessment about commercial bank supervisory policies. The authors identify which policies ease or intensify the degree to which bank corruption is an obstacle to firms raising external finance. They found that especially one supervisory strategy can lead to a decrease of corruption of bank officials. This supervisory strategy focuses on empowering private monitoring of banks, which forces the banks to disclose accurate information to the private sector.

Finally, Boyd *et al.* (2001) examine the impact of inflation on the aggregate financial sector. He found that inflation hinders financial development in the sense that there is a negative relationship between inflation and both stock market development and banking sector activity. Bennaceur and Ghazouani (2005) extends the work of Boyd *et al.* (2001) and describes the influence of inflation on the financial sector performance in the MENA region. He also states that inflation has a negative and significant incidence on financial sector development. However, there is no evidence of threshold levels. The authors show that a marginal increase of inflation is harmless to stock market performance and banking sector development, regardless of the inflation rate, which for Morocco is relatively low. The rate of 1% in 2010 was mainly due to an accelerated rise in volatile food prices (BAM, 2010).

5 Conclusion

This study compares MFBs in terms of their institutional development. The data analysis conducted in this master's thesis indicates the possible institutional development of the MCAs. Moroccan institutions also intend to transform from a NGO into a regulated MFB. The two analyses compare the different institutions before and after their legal status transition. The comparison of the MCAs and former NGOs shows differences between the institutions. The MCAs are more developed in terms of institutional size and financial performance than the former NGOs. In turn, two of the NGOs are stronger in terms of outreach. Therefore, the MCAs already show typical characteristics of sustainable MFBs. The second comparative analysis shows similarities between the selected MFBs after their transformation. Their experiences can be applicable to the MCAs in order to predict the latter's future development.

To answer the first research question, the MCAs' assets, clients, staff, and average loan balances may increase further. Their outreach can rise, at least in terms of depth and scope. Their financial performance can also increase after the transformation but not in the long-term. Corporate governance structures may not experience severe changes. Their owner structure will probably concentrate on development agencies, local investors, and those investors who seek financial return and social effects at the same time. To answer the second research question, regulatory changes are necessary to allow such a transformation. Until the beginning of 2012, the Microcredit Associations Law has prevented MCAs to transform into MFBs. However, their macroeconomic environment is suitable for the institutions' growth.

There is no clear answer to the question of whether such a transformation makes sense for the MCAs or not. Even though the findings of this thesis are widely positive, they do not imply that the institutions should be transformed into regulated FIs. Fernando (2004) states that the institutional transformation of NGOs should not be viewed as the only approach to sustainable microfinance. However, what the MCAs can learn from other MFBs is that the transformation allows for access to new funding sources and further institutional growth.

The limitations of this study are the low number of MFIs in the comparative analyses (see Chapter 4). The sample of former NGOs which finally transform into a MFB can be extended because there are MFIs which transform into MFBs and do not provide data to the MIX dataset. Furthermore, the data in the MIX dataset is partly not complete, and other datasets might have data samples with more reporting years which include the foundation, the transformation point of time, and thereafter. Moreover, most of the MFBs in the second comparative analysis are from the LAC region (10 out of 16) and that can have an impact on the results as the PCBs are also located in Latin-America (see Chapter 4.2.1). In addition, the comparison implies that the banks have comparable values independently of their operating experience and their calculated mean values. But the transformation dates of the banks are different, and all MCAs and MFBs rather differ in terms of their calculated mean values (see Tables 8, 9, 10, and 11). Finally, the results of the normality test in Chapter 4.2.1 are positive.

Bibliography

ACLEDA BANK PLC (2012). Annual report. *Association of Cambodian Local Economic Development Agencies Bank Plc.*

AHLIN, C., LIN, J. and MAIO, M. (2011). Where does microfinance fourish? Microfinance institution performance in macroeconomic context. *Journal of Development Economics*, **95** (2), 105–120.

AL AMANA (2010). Al Amana MICROFINANCE. *http://www.alamana.org.ma/*, visited on 03-02-2012.

ALEXANDER, H. (2005). *Sustainable Microfinance Banks - IMI as a Public-Private Partnership in Practice*, Springer-Verlag, KfW Entwicklungsbank, chap. 25, pp. 289–296.

ALLAIRE, V., ASHTA, A., ATTUEL-MENDES, L. and KRISHNASWAMY, K. (2009). Institutional Analysis to Explain the Success of Moroccan Microfinance Institutions. *Cahier du CEREN*, **29**, 6–26.

AMHA, W. (2004). Managing growth of microfinance institutions (MFIs): Balancing sustainability and reaching large number of clients in Ethiopia. *Ethiopian Journal of Economics*, **13** (2), 61–101.

ARMENDÁRIZ, B. and MORDUCH, J. (2010). *The Economics of Microfinance.* Cambridge and London: MIT Press.

ASFI (2011). Evaluacíon del sistema financiero al 30 de septiembre de 2011. *Autoridad de Supervisi6n del Sistema Financiero Bolivio.*

ATALLAH, C. and EL HYANI, O. (2009). *Microfinance: Quelles perspectives de développement pour les IMF - Cas du Maroc*. Master's thesis, ESCP Europe.

AUBERT, D. J. A., C. and SADOULET, E. (2009). Designing credit agent incentives to prevent mission drift in pro-poor microfinance institutions. *Journal of Development Economics*, **90**, 153–62.

BAM (2010). *Annual Report*. Bank Al-Maghrib.

BANCO ADOPEM (2008). Asociación Dominicana para el Desarrollo de la Mujer: Banco de Ahorro y Crédito. *http://www.bancoadopem.com*, visited on 02-20-2012.

BANEX (2010). Banco del exito. *https://www.banex.com.ni/*, visited on 03-01-2012.

BÉDÉCARRATS, F., BASTIAENSEN, J. and DOLIGEZ, F. (2012). Co-optation, Cooperation or Competition? Microfinance and the new left in Bolivia, Ecuador and Nicaragua. *Third World Quarterly*, **33** (1), 143–160.

BECK, T., DEMIRGÜÇ-KUNT, A., and LEVINE, R. (2006). Bank supervision and corruption in lending. *Journal of Monetary Economics*, **53**, 2131–2163.

—, DEMIRGUÇ-KUNT, A. and LEVINE, R. (2010). Financial Institutions and Markets across Countries and over Time: The Updated Financial Development and Structure Database. *The World Bank Economic Review*, **24** (1), 77–92.

—, — and LEVINE, R. E. (2000). A New Database on Financial Development and Structure. *World Bank Economic Review, http://econ.worldbank.org/*, **14**, 597–605, visited on 02-25-2012.

BENNACEUR, S., BEN-KHEDHIRI, H. and CASU, B. (2011). *What Drives the Performance of Selected MENA Banks? A Meta-Frontier Analysis*. Tech. rep., International Monetary Fund WP/11/34, visited on 02-27-2012.

— and GHAZOUANI, S. (2005). Does Inflation Impact on Financial Sector Performance in the MENA Region? *Review of Middle East Economics and Finance*, **3** (3), 219–229.

BERA, A. K. and JARQUE, C. M. (1980). Efficient tests for normality, homoscedasticity and serial independence of regression residuals. *Economics Letters*, **6** (3), 255–259.

BOYD, J. H., LEVINE, R. and SMITH, B. D. (2001). The impact of inflation on financial sector performance. *Journal of Monetary Economics*, **47** (2), 221–248.

BRYS, G., HUBERT, M. and STRUYF, A. (2004). *A robustification of the Jarque-Bera test of normality*, Springer, Berlin, Germany, pp. 753–760.

CALDÉRON, T. B. (2006). *Micro-bubble or Micro-immunity? Risk and Return in Microfinance: Lessons from recent Crisis in Latin America*, Springer-Verlag, KfW Entwicklungsbank, chap. 4, pp. 65–75.

CAMPION, A. and WHITE, V. (1999). *Institutional metamorphosis: transformation of microfinance NGOs into regulated financial institutions*. Occasional Paper No. 4, MicroFinance Network, Washington, DC: Distributed by PACT Publications.

— and — (2001). NGO Transformation. *Betsheda, Microenterprise Best Practices: 31*.

CEPAL (2011). *Anuario estadístico de América Latina y el Caribe*. Naciones Unidas.

CGAP (2005). Caja Los Andes (Bolivia) Diversifies into Rural Lending. *CGAP Agricultural Microfinance, Case Study No. 3, Washington, DC.*

— (2009). Turning Principles into Practice. *CGAP Microfinance Gateway, Washington DC.*

— (2011). What Is a Microfinance Institution (MFI)? *Consultative Group to Assist the Poor: Advancing financial access for the world's poor, Washington, DC.*

CHEN, G., RASMUSSEN, S. and REILLE, X. (2010). Growth and Vulnerabilities in Microfinance. *CGAP Focus Note No. 61, Washington, DC.*

CHRISTEN, R. (2000). Commercialization and mission drift, the transformation of microfinance in Latin America. *CGAP Occasional Paper No. 5, Washington, DC.*

CHRISTEN, R. P. (2001). Commercialization and mission drift: The transformation of microfinance in latin america. *CGAP Occasional paper No. 5, Washington DC.*

COHEN, M. and GOODWIN-GROEN, R. (2004). The Story of Al Amana: Morocco. *Microfinance Gateway, CGAP, Washington, DC.*

CULL, R., DEMIRGUÇ-KUNT, A. and MORDUCH, J. (2007). Financial performance and outreach: A global analysis of lending microbanks. *The Economic Journal*, **117** (1), 107–133.

—, — and — (2009). *Microfinance meets the market.* Policy Research Working Paper Series 4630, The World Bank, visited on 03-12-2012.

DE SOUSA-SHIELDS, M. (2006). *Commercial Investment in Microfinance: A Class by Itself?*, Springer-Verlag, KfW Entwicklungsbank, chap. 6, pp. 81–94.

DEMIRGÜÇ-KUNT, A. and DETRAGIACHE, E. (1998). Financial Liberalization and Financial Fragility. *Paper prepared for the Annual World Bank Conference on Development Economics, Washington, D.C.*

DICHTER, T. (2007). A Second Look at Microfinance. The Sequence of Growth and Credit in Economic History. *Development Briefing Paper*, (1).

DIECKMANN, R. (2007). Microfinance: An emerging investment opportunity. *Deutsche Bank Research, Frankfurt, Germany.*

— (2008). Microfinance: An attractive dual return investment opportunity. *Deutsche Bank Research, Frankfurt, Germany.*

FBPMC (2010). Annual report. *Fondation Banque Populaire de Micro-Crédit.*

FERNANDO, N. A. (2004). Micro Success Story? Transformation of Non-government Organizations Into Regulated Financial Institutions. *Asian Development Bank.*

FISMAN, R. and SVENSSON, J. (2007). Are corruption and taxation really harmful to growth? Firm-level evidence. *Journal of Development Economics*, **83** (1), 63–75.

FNAM (2012). Fédération Nationale des Associations de Microcrédit. *http://www.fnam.ma/*, visited on 03-08-2012.

FONDEP (2011). Fondation pour le Dévelopment Local et le Partenariat. *http://www.fondep.com/*, visited on 02-18-2012.

FREYTAG, C. (2005). *Degrees of Competition in Serving Target Groups - They May Be Closer than You Think*, Springer-Verlag, KfW Entwicklungsbank, chap. 20, pp. 233–237.

GIZ (2004). Measuring the Impact of Micro Finance: The Case of Financiera Calpiá, El Salvador. *Deutsche Gesellschaft für Internationale Zusammenarbeit GmbH, Abteilung 41 Finanzsystementwicklung.*

GONZALEZ, A. (2007). Resilience of microfinance institutions to national macroeconomic events: An econometric analysis of MFI asset quality. *MIX Discussion Paper No. 1.*

GUTIERREZ-GOIRIA, J. and GOITISOLO LEZAMA, B. (2011). Profitability and Social Performance of Microfinance Institutions: Empirical Evidence of Relations between Different Types of Variables. *Revista de Economía Mundial*, **27**, 189–214.

HARMELING, S. and AUSTIN, J. E. (2000). Women's World Banking: Catalytic Change Through Networks. *HBS Case No. 9-300-050, Harvard Business School Publishing, Boston, Massachusetts.*

HARRENDORF, S., HEISKANEN, M. and MALBY, S. (2010). International Statistics on Crime and Justice. *European Institute for Crime Prevention and Control (HEUNI) and United Nations Office on Drugs and Crime (UNODC).*

HARTARSKA, V. and NADOLNYAK, D. (2007). Do regulated microfinance institutions achieve better sustainability and outreach? Cross-country evidence. *Applied Economics*, **39** (10), 1207–1222.

—, PARMETER, C. F. and NADOLNYAK, D. (2011). Economies of Scope of Lending and Mobilizing Deposits in Microfinance Institutions: Asemiparametric Analysis. *American Journal of Agricultural Economics*, **93** (2), 389–398.

HASHEMI, S. and ROSENBERG, R. (2006). Graduating the poor into mircofinance: Linking safety nets and ?nancial services. *CGAP Focus note No. 34, Washington, DC.*

HERMES, N., LENSINK, R. and MEESTERS, A. (2008). Outreach and Efficiency of Microfinance Institutions. *International Review of Economics Finance*, **17** (4), 558–571.

HISAKO, K. (2009). Competition and wide outreach of microfinance institutions. *Economics Bulletin*, **29**, 2628–2639.

HISHIGSUREN, G. (2006). Transformation of Micro-finance Operations from NGO to Regulated MFI. *Microfinance Gateway, CGAP, Washington, DC.*

HONOHAN, P. and BECK, T. (2007). Making Finance Work for Africa. *The World Bank, Washington, D.C.*

IMAI, K., GAIHA, R., THAPA, G., GUPTA, S. K. A. and GUPTA, A. (2011). *Performance of Microfinance Institutions: A Macroeconomic and Institutional Perspective*. The School of Economics Discussion Paper Series 1116, Economics, The University of Manchester, visited on 03-18-2012.

IMF (2008). Morocco: Financial System Stability Assessment Update. *IMF Country Report 08/333.*

ISERN, J. and PORTEOUS, D. (2005). Commercial banks and microfinance: Evolving models of success. *CGAP Focus Note No. 28, Washington, DC.*

JAÏDA (2011). Enquête sectorielle 2010: Analyse du prêt individuel et de lendettement croisé. *JAÏDA Groupe CDG: Fonds des financements des organismes de Microfinance au Maroc.*

JANSSON, T. (2003). Financing microfinance. *IDB Technical Paper, Sustainable Development Department, Washington, DC.*

JEGEDE, C. A., KEHINDE, J. and AKINLABI, B. H. (2011). Impact of microfinance on poverty alleviation in nigeria: An empirical investigation. *European Journal of Humanities and Social Sciences*, **2** (1).

KAPOOR, M., RAVI, S. and MORDUCH, J. (2007). From microfinance to microfinance. Innovations: Technology, Governance. *Globalization*, **2** (1-2), 82–90.

KARLAN, D. S. and ZINMAN, J. (2008). Credit Elasticities in Less-Developed Economies: Implications for Microfinance. *American Economic Review*, **98** (3), 1040–1068.

KHANAL, D. R. (2007). *Banking and insurance services liberalization and development in Bangladesh, Nepal and Malaysia: A comparative analysis*. Tech. rep., Asia-Pacific Research and Training Network on Trade, Working Paper Series, No. 41, visited on 03-03-2012.

KING, R. G. and LEVINE, R. (1993). Finance and Growth: Schumpeter Might Be Right. *The Quarterly Journal of Economics*, **108** (3), 717–737.

KRAUSS, N. and WALTER, I. (2008). *Can Microfinance Reduce Portfolio Volatility?* Tech. rep., NYU Working Paper No. FIN-07-054, visited on 26-12-2011.

LAUER, K. (2008). Transforming NGO MFIs: Critical Ownership Issues to Consider. *CGAP Occasional Paper No. 13, Washington, DC*, **13**.

L'ÉCONOMISTE (2005). Microcredit: Vous avez des hommes qui ont placé le barre haut. *L'Économiste, Édition N° 1975 du 10/03/2005*.

L'ÉCONOMISTE (2007). SFI-Microfinance : Le Maroc, un cas d'école. *L'Économiste, Édition N° 2571 du 17/07/2007*.

LEDGERWOOD, J. (1998). *Microfinance handbook: An institutional and financial perspective*. Sustainable Banking with the Poor Series, World Bank Publications, Washington D.C., USA.

LUOTO, J., MCINTOSH, C. and WYDICK, B. (2007). Credit Information Systems in Less Developed Countries: A Test with Microfinance in Guatemala. *Economic Development and Cultural Change*, **55** (2), 313–334.

M-CRIL (2008). Nepal rural development society centre (nrdsc). *Micro-Finance Rating*.

MANOS, R. and YARON, J. (2009). Key issues in assessing the performance of microfinance institutions. *Canadian Journal of Development Studies*, **29**, 101–122.

MAURYA, R. (2011). Women, Microfinance and Financial Inclusion in India. *International Journal of Business Economics and Research Management Research*, **2** (7).

MCKIM, A. and HUGHART, M. (2005). Staff incentive schemes in practice: findings from a global survey of microfinance institutions. *CGAP, Microfinance Network, Washington, DC.*

MERSLAND, R. and ØYSTEIN STRØM, R. (2008). Performance and Trade-offs in Microfinance Organisations - Does ownership matter? *Journal of International Development*, **20**, 598–612.

— and — (2009). Performance and governance in microfinance institutions. *Journal of Banking & Finance*, **33**, 662–669.

MIXMARKET (2010). Microfinance data and Social Performance measurements for the microfinance institutions. *Microfinance Information Exchange Inc., http://www.mixmarket.org/*, visited on 03-20-2012.

MIXMARKET (2010). Mix market glossary. *Microfinance Information Exchange Inc., http://www.mixmarket.org/about/faqs/glossary*, visited on 02-21-2012.

MONTGOMERY, H. and WEISS, J. (2005). Great expectations: microfinance and poverty reduction in Asia and Latin America. *Oxford Development Studies*, **33**, 391–416.

MORDUCH, J. (1999). The microfinance promise. *Journal of Economic Literature*, **37**, 1569–1614.

— (2000). The microfinance schism. *World Development*, **28**, 617–629.

NAVAJAS, S., SCHREINER, M. and MEYER, R. L. (2000). Microcredit and the Poorest of the Poor: Theory and Evidence from Bolivia. *World Development*, **28** (2), 333–346.

NGUYEN, J. (2011). Market Concentration and other Determinants of Bank Profitability: Evidence from Panel Data. *International Research Journal of Finance and Economics*, **70**.

OKOJIE, C. E. E., MONYE-EMINA, A., EGHAFONA, K., OSAGHAE, G. and EHIAKHAMEN, J. (2009). Institutional Environment and Access to Microfinance By Self-employed Women in the Rural Areas of Edo State, Nigeria. *Nigeria Strategy Support Program (NSSP), Background Paper No. NSSP 003*.

OLSEN, T. D. (2010). New Actors in Microfinance Lending: The Role of Regulation and Competition in Latin America. *Perspectives on Global Development and Technology*, **9**, 500–519.

PCB BOLIVIA (2010). *Annual Report*. ProCredit Bank Bolivia.

PCB EL SALVADOR (2010). *Annual Report*. ProCredit Bank El Salvador.

PCH (2010). *Annual Report*. ProCredit Holding.

POLLINGER, J. J., OUTHWAITE, J. and CORDERO-GUZMÁN, H. (2007). The Question of Sustainability for Microfinance Institutions. *Journal of Small Business Management*, **45** (1), 23–41.

QUAYES, S. (2011). Depth of outreach and financial sustainability of microfinance institutions. *Applied Economics*, **26** (1), 1–13.

REILLE, X. (2009). The Rise, Fall, and Recovery of the Microfinance Sector in Morocco. *BRIEF, CGAP, Washington, DC*.

— (2010). Unsustainable Growth. *Microfinance Gateway, CGAP, Washington, DC*.

—, FORSTER, S. and ROZAS, D. (2011). Foreign Capital Investment in Microfinance: Reassessing Financial and Social Returns. *CGAP Focus Note No. 71, Washington, DC.*

— and LYMAN, T. R. (2005). Diagnostic Report on the Legal and Regulatory Environment for Microfinance in Morocco. *Microfinance Gateway, CGAP, Washington, DC.*

REINERT, A. (2011). Anlegen fernab vom launischen Markt. *Handelsblatt 31.01.2012.*

RHYNE, E. and OTERO, E. (2006). Microfinance through the next decade: Visioning the who, what where, when and how. *Paper commissioned by the Global Microcredit Summit 2006, ACCION International, Boston, Massachusetts.*

RHYNE, F. (1998). The Yin and Yang of microfinance: reaching the poor and sustainability. *Microbank Bulletin*, **2**, 6–8.

ROSENBERG, R. (2007). Reflections on the Compartamos Initial Public Offering: A Case Study on Microfinance Interest Rates and Profits. *CGAP Focus Note No. 42, Washington, DC.*

SCHICKS, J. (2010). *Microfinance Over-Indebtedness: Understanding its drivers and challenging the common myths*. Working Papers CEB 10-048, ULB - Universite Libre de Bruxelles, visited on 01-25-2012.

SCHMIDT, R. and WINKLER, A. (2000). Building Financial Institutions in Developing Countries. *Journal für Entwicklungspolitik*, **16** (3), 329–346.

SCHMIDT, R. H. (2005). Die Sicht der teilnehmenden Beobachter: Ein Abriss der IPC/IMI-Geschichte aus neoinstitutionalistischer Perspektive. In B. Fritz and K. Hujo (eds.), *Ökonomie unter den Bedingungen Lateinamerikas*, Frankfurt am Main: Vervuert, pp. 95–122.

— (2010). Microfinance, Commercialization and Ethics. *Poverty & Public Policy*, **2** (1).

SCHREINER, M. (2002). Aspects of outreach: A framework for discussion of the social benefits of microfinance. *Journal of International Development*, **14**, 591–603.

SEELKE, C. R. (2011). Gangs in central america. *Congressional Research Paper*.

SHARMA, M. P. (2004). Community-driven development and scaling-up of microfinance services: case studies from Nepal and India. *FCND Discussion Paper No. 178*.

SUMSER, H. M. (2008). *ADOPEM Bank - Microfinance in the Dominican Republic, A case study*. Master's thesis, The Fletcher School, Tufts University.

TERBERGER, E. (2003). Microfinance institutions in the development of financial markets. *CEPAL Review*, **81**, 187–202.

THAPA, G. (2007). Sustainability and Governance of Microfinance Institutions: Recent Experiences and Some Lessons for Southeast Asia. *Asian Journal of Agriculture and Development*, **4** (1).

THE ECONOMIST (2011). The tormented isthmus: Big-time drug trafficking has arrived in Central America. Its poor, politically polarised countries must now try to cope. *The Economist Newspaper Limited*.

VANROOSE, A. (2007). The Transformation of Microfinance Institutions: Beneficial for the Poor? *Preliminary version, Paper to be presented at the Conference on Poverty and Capital Manchester, 2-4 July 2007*.

WAGNER, C. (2011). *From Boom to Bust: How different has Microfinance been from traditional banking?* Tech. rep., Frankfurt School of Finance and Management, visited on 01-10-2012.

WOLLER, G. (2002). The promise and peril of microfinance commercialization. *Small Enterprise Journal*, **13** (4), 12–21.

WORLD BANK (2011). Crime and Violence in Central America: A Development Challenge. *Sustainable Development Department and Poverty Reduction and Economic Management Unit, Latin America and the Caribbean Region.*

ZEITINGER, C.-P. (2004). *Sustainable Microfinance Banks - Problems and Perspectives*, Springer-Verlag, KfW Entwicklungsbank, chap. 10, pp. 125–134.

A Tables

Table 1: Financial development indicators for Morocco and the MENA Region

		2005	2006	2007	2008	2009
Liquid Liabilities/	Morocco	0.84	0.90	0.97	1.06	1.14
GDP	MENA	0.63	0.64	0.71	0.73	0.76
	Lower Middle Income	0.47	0.47	0.49	0.54	0.58
	High Income	0.88	0.91	0.98	1.03	1.07
Financial System Deposits/	Morocco	0.68	0.72	0.78	0.86	0.95
GDP	MENA	0.52	0.52	0.60	0.63	0.66
	Lower Middle Income	0.39	0.39	0.42	0.46	0.50
	High Income	0.85	0.88	0.95	0.99	1.03
Bank Credit/	Morocco	0.73	0.74	0.81	0.89	1.00
Bank Deposits	MENA	0.52	0.52	0.53	0.53	0.54
	Lower Middle Income	0.78	0.78	0.83	0.88	0.94
	High Income	1.16	1.19	1.18	1.24	1.31
Stock Market Capitalization/	Morocco	0.45	0.59	0.86	1.24	1.84
GDP	MENA	0.65	0.76	0.77	0.81	0.91
	Lower Middle Income	0.33	0.40	0.50	0.60	0.72
	High Income	0.93	1.01	1.12	1.26	1.47

Source: Financial Development and Structure Database as of 12/2011

Table 2: Banking sector assets for Morocco and the MENA Region

		2005	2006	2007	2008	2009
Net Interest Margin	Morocco	0.03	0.03	0.03	0.03	0.03
	MENA	0.03	0.03	0.03	0.04	0.04
	Lower Middle Income	0.05	0.05	0.5	0.06	0.06
	High Income	0.03	0.03	0.03	0.03	0.03
Bank Concentration	Morocco	0.66	0.66	0.78	0.91	1.00
	MENA	0.73	0.73	0.72	0.75	0.78
	Lower Middle Income	0.67	0.64	0.65	0.67	0.69
	High Income	0.69	0.70	0.72	0.76	0.79
Bank Return on Assets	Morocco	0.00	0.01	0.01	0.01	0.01
	MENA	0.01	0.01	0.01	0.03	0.07
	Lower Middle Income	0.00	0.02	0.01	-0.03	-3.03
	High Income	0.02	0.02	0.02	0.02	0.10
Bank Return on Equity	Morocco	-0.28	0.16	0.18	0.20	0.22
	MENA	0.05	0.13	0.15	0.13	0.33
	Lower Middle Income	0.11	0.14	0.12	0.11	-0.17
	High Income	0.14	0.15	0.15	0.16	0.21
Bank Cost-Income Ratio	Morocco	0.66	0.55	0.48	0.42	0.36
	MENA	0.49	0.54	0.50	0.47	0.47
	Lower Middle Income	0.67	0.67	0.64	0.64	0.61
	High Income	0.58	0.59	0.57	0.59	0.64

Source: Financial Development and Structure Database as of 12/2011

Table 3: List of the microcredit associations in Morocco

Year of foundation	Name of the Moroccan Microcredit Association
1994	Association Marocaine de Solidarité Sans Frontières (AMSSF/MC)
1996	Fondation pour le Développement Local et le Partenariat (FONDEP)
1997	Al Amana Microfinance
1998	Fondation Banque Populaire pour le Microcrédit (FBPMC)
1998	Association Ismailia pour le Microcrédit (AIMC)
1999	Fondation Al Karama pour le Microcrédit
1999	Institution Marocaine d'Appui à la Micro-Entreprise (INMAA)
2000	Association de Microfinance Oued Srou (AMOS)
2001	L'Association Tétouanaise des Initiatives Socioprofessionnelle de Microcrédit (ATIL Micro Crédit)
2001	Fondation ARDI (ex Fondation Crédit Agricole pour le Microcrédit)
2003	Fondation Microcrédit du Nord
2009	Association TAWADA pour le Microcrédit

Source: Fédération Nationale des Associations de Microcrédit as of 02/2012

Table 4: Moroccan microfinance sector dominating the MENA region as of 12/2010

	Participating MFIs		Active Borrowers		Loan Portfolio (in USD)	
	Number	Percent	Number	Percent	Number	Percent
Morocco	8	16.33%	807,090	59.21%	570,251,144	95.75%
Rest of MENA	49	83.67%	1,363,125	40.79%	595,582,285	4.25%
Total	57	100.00%	2,170,215	100.00%	1,165,833,429	100.00%

Source: MIX dataset as of 01/2012

Table 5: Maturities and interest rates of borrowings in the MENA Region as of 12/2010

Lender Type	Interest rate (%)	Maturity (months)
Egypt	9.96%	22
Iraq	4.96%	24
Jordan	7.37%	59
Lebanon	4.73%	60
Morocco	4.77%	82
Palestine	2.67%	45
Yemen	10.31%	35

Source: MIX dataset as of 01/2012

Table 6: Basic figures on the three largest microcredit associations as of 12/2010

	Al Amana	FBPMC	FONDEP
Gross Loan Portfolio (in USD)	295,347,932	154,140,275	80,825,115
Number of active borrowers	339,408	193,998	132,431
Portfolio at risk > 30 days	7.84%	4.16%	2.37%
Operational self-sufficiency	102.32%	134.55%	135.11%
Return on equity	3.27%	15.27%	33.52%

Source: MIX dataset as of 01/2012

Table 7: Indicators for the analysis of microfinance institutions

Institutional Area	Indicator
Institutional size	Assets Number of employees Number of branches
Financial Performance	Operational Self-sufficiency Return on assets Return on equity PAR > 30 days Write-off ratio Yield on gross loan portfolio
Funding structure	Equity over assets Deposits over assets Borrowings over assets
Outreach	*Depth of outreach* Average loan balance per borrower *Outreach to female borrowers* Number of female borrowers/total borrowers *Breath of outreach* Number of total clients *Scope of outreach* Number of types of financial contracts
Financial Intermediation	Deposits over loan portfolio

Table 8: Comparison of the MCAs 3 years before their possible transformation (in USD)

	Al Amana		FBPMC		FONDEP	
	Change	Mean	Change	Mean	Change	Mean
Assets	-14%	367,039,777	7%	157,474,438	0%	91,812,811
Employees	2%	2,110	-21%	845	-10%	908
No. of active borrowers	-28%	404,374	9%	172,811	-4%	127,074
Average loan balance per borrower	23%	814	8%	797	16%	551
Percent of female borrowers	-11%	42%	10%	54%	-9%	57%
Operational self sufficiency	-1%	103%	2%	129%	9%	114%
Return on assets	-29%	1%	28%	5%	27%	2%
Portfolio at risk > 30 days	110%	6%	39%	4%	-4%	4%

Source: MIX dataset as of 02/2012

Table 9: Comparison of former NGOs 3 years before their transformation (in USD)

	ADOPEM		D-Miro		Nirdhan		Nerude	
	Change	Mean	Change	Mean	Change	Mean	Change	Mean
Assets	-9%	17,507,595	35%	28,119,116	179%	981,691	195%	1,199,145
Employees			-8%	196	196%	88	138%	67
No. of active borrowers	47%	35,374	1%	33,999	220%	5,426	105%	13,839
Average loan balance per borrower	-45%	292	21%	723	-12%	70	17%	63
Percent of female borrowers			-8%	65%	0%	100%	0%	100%
Operational self sufficiency			-19%	94%	-1%	56%	-15%	97%
Return on assets			-404%	-2%			-216%	-1%
Portfolio at risk > 30 days			62%	4%			438%	1%

Source: MIX dataset as of 02/2012

Table 10: Comparison of transformed MFBs 3 years after the transformation (in USD) [1]

	ACLEDA	ADOPEM	Comp.	K-Rep	MiBanco
Assets	143,727,407	30,392,419	450,813,456	16,226,021	47,574,045
Average loan balance per borrower	747	354	416	427	617
Number of active borrowers	141,008	60,660	870,377	23,095	59,125
OSS	125%	146%	175%	123%	116%
Percent of female borrowers	63%	80%	98%	52%	58%
Employees	2,422	284	4,475	162	471
Portfolio at risk > 30 days	1%	4%	2%	3%	2%
ROA	4%	10%	20%	2%	4%

Source: MIX dataset as of 02/2012

Table 11: Comparison of transformed MFBs 3 years after the transformation (in USD) [2]

Assets	Nirdhan	NRDSC	OBM	PCB Bolivia	PCB El Salvador
Average loan balance per borrower	4,078,958	5,101,827	39,489,675	343,204,883	175,761,000
Number of active borrowers	79	117	3,285	2,795	1,986
OSS	28,922	34,848	8,362	94,446	66,730
Percent of female borrowers	85%	133%	119%	109%	112%
Employees	100%	100%	40%	44%	32%
Portfolio at risk > 30 days	212	151	84	1,400	752
ROA	6%	0%	1%	2%	3%
	-3%	2%	3%	1%	1%

Source: MIX dataset as of 02/2012

Table 12: Transformation development of the selected microfinance banks

Year of foundation	NGO Name	Year of FI transformation	FI Name	Year of Bank transformation	Bank Name
1911	Círculo de Obreros	1991	Banco Caja Social (Savings Bank)	2005	Caja Social BCSC
1969	Acción Comunitaria del Perú			1998	MiBanco
1977	Bancamía			2008	Bancamía S.A.
1982	ADOPEM			2004	Banco ADOPEM
1983	ADEMI			1998	Banco ADEMI
1984	PRODEM			1992	BancoSol
1984	K-Rep			1999	K-Rep Bank
1985	FIE ONG	1998	Fondo Financiero FFP	2009	Banco Fie
1988	AMPES	1995	Financiera CALPIA	2004	PCB El Salvador
1990	Compartamos NGO	2000	Financiera Compartamos	2006	Compartamos Banco
1991	Nirdhan			1999	Nirdhan Utthan Bank Ltd
1992	Procrédito	1995	Caja Los Andes	2005	PCB Bolivia
1993	NRDSC			2007	Nerude Bank Ltd
1993	ACLEDA[a]	2000	ACLEDA (specialized bank)	2003	ACLEDA Bank Plc.
1993	FINDESA	2002	FINDESA	2008	BANEX
1996	D-Miro			2011	D-Miro
1997	Constanta	2007	JSC Constanta	2008	JSC Bank Constanta
1999	Microcredit Montenegro			2002	Erste Bank Podgorica (OBM)

Source: Information published on MIXMarket & the banks' publications as of 02/2012

a In 1995, ACLEDA transformed into a fully self-financing MFI specialised in providing financial services to the lower segments of the market.

Table 13: Location of the selected microfinance banks

Bank Name	Region	Country	City
Caja Social BCSC	LAC	Colomia	Bogotá
MiBanco	LAC	Peru	Lima
Bancamía S.A.	LAC	Colomia	Bogotá
Banco ADOPEM	LAC	Dom. Republic	Santo Domingo
Banco ADEMI	LAC	Dom. Republic	Santo Domingo
BancoSol	LAC	Bolivia	La Paz
K-Rep Bank	Africa	Kenya	Nairobi
Banco Fie	LAC	Bolivia	La Paz
PCB El Salvador	LAC	El Salvador	San Salvador
Compartamos Banco	LAC	Mexico	Mexico City
Nirdhan Utthan Bank Ltd	South Asia	Nepal	Siddarthanagar
PCB Bolivia	LAC	Bolivia	Santa Cruz
Nerude Laghubitta Bikas Bank Ltd	South Asia	Nepal	Biratnagar
ACLEDA Bank Plc.	EAP	Cambodia	Phnom Phen
BANEX	LAC	Nicaragua	Managua
D-Miro	LAC	Ecuador	Guayas
JSC Bank Constanta	EECA	Georgia	Tbilisi
Erste Bank AD Podgorica (OBM)	EECA	Montenegro	Podgorica

Source: Information published on MIXMarket & the banks' publications as of 02/2012

Table 14: Other MFIs transforming into microfinance banks

Year of foundation	MFI Name	Year of first stage transformation	MFI Name	Year of bank transformation	Bank Name
1967	Empresa Crédito Familiar	1992	Financiera Familiar	2008	Banco Familiar
1976			Teba Savings Fund	2000	SA Reserve Bank
1980	Trust company	1983	Trust FI	1993	Centenary Bank
1984			KAFC	2006	Aiyl Bank
1986			Family Finance Building Society	2007	Family Bank Limited
1992			SOCREMO project	2003	Socremo Banco
1993			FORA Fund	2005	CJSC FORUS Bank
1994			Fundusz Mikro	2010	FM Bank
1995			FEFAD	2003	PCB Albania
1997			Uganda Microfinance Limited	2008	Equity Bank
1998	XAC LLC	1998	XAC LLC	2001	XAC Bank
1999			ProCredit Moldova	2008	PCB Moldova
2000			Financiara CONFIA	2005	PCB Nicaragua
2001			Sociedad Financiera Ecuatorial S.A.	2005	PCB Ecuador
2007			ProCredit Colombia S.A.	2008	PCB Colombia

Source: Information published on MIXMarket & the banks' publications as of 02/2012

Table 15: Location of other MFIs transforming into microfinance banks

Bank Name	Region	Country	City
Banco Familiar	LAC	Paraguay	Asuncion
SA Reserve Bank	Africa	South Africa	Johannesburg
Centenary Bank	Africa	Uganda	Kampala
Aiyl Bank	EECA	Kyrgyzstan	Bishkek
Family Bank Limited	Africa	Kenya	Nairobi
Socremo: Banco de Microfinanças	Africa	Mozambique	Maputo
CJSC FORUS Bank	EECA	Russia	Nizhni Novgorod
FM Bank	EECA	Poland	Warsaw
PCB Albania	EECA	Albania	Tirana
Equity Bank	Africa	Uganda	Kampala
XAC Bank	EECA	Mongolia	Ulaanbaatar
PCB Moldova	EECA	Moldova	Chisinau
PCB Nicaragua	LAC	Nicaragua	Managua
PCB Ecuador	LAC	Ecuador	Quito
PCB Colombia	LAC	Colombia	Bogotá

Source: Information published on MIXMarket & the banks' publications as of 02/2012

Table 16: Profitability of microfinance institutions in 2010

Institution type	Number of MFIs	For-profit status	Percent profitable	Number of active borrowers	Number of borrowers served by for-profit MFIs	Percent served by for-profit MFIs
Bank	94	91	97%	28,027,581	19,800,355	71%
Credit Union / Cooperative	152	3	2%	1,963,273	40,919	2%
NBFI	393	313	80%	39,084,927	37,013,071	95%
NGO	424	0	0%	30,649,456	0	0%
Rural Bank	38	38	100%	1,083,558	1,083,558	100%
Total	1101	445	40%	100,808,795	57,937,903	57%

Source: MIX dataset as of 02/2012

Table 17: Profitability of microfinance institutions in 2000

Institution type	Number of MFIs	For-profit status	Percent profitable	Number of active borrowers	Number of borrowers served by for-profit MFIs	Percent served by for-profit MFIs
Bank	28	27	96%	3,332,666	3,331,008	100%
Credit Union / Cooperative	18	0	0%	168,067	0	0%
NBFI	61	47	77%	1,224,376	868,226	71%
NGO	88	0	0%	6,032,627	0	0%
Rural Bank	4	4	100%	37,685	37,685	100%
Total	199	78	39%	10,795,421	4,236,919	39%

Source: MIX dataset as of 02/2012

Table 18: PCB El Salvador - Shareholder structure

Shareholder (as of December 31, 2010)	Sector	Headquarters	Share	Paid-in Capital (in thousands of USD)
ProCredit Holding	Investment	Germany	99.65%	20,179.50
FUNDASAL	Housing	El Salvador	0.07%	14.5
Others			0.28%	56
Total Capital			100%	20,250.00

Source: PCB El Salvador, Annual Report 2010

Table 19: PCB Bolivia - Shareholder structure

Shareholders (as of December 31, 2010)	Sector	Headquarters	Share	Paid-in Capital (in USD)
ProCredit Holding	Investment	Germany	99.96%	45,488,401
Other	Various		0.04%	16,657
Total			100%	45,505,058

Source: PCB Bolivia, Annual Report 2010

Table 20: JSC Bank Constanta - Shareholder structure

Shareholders (as of November 2011)	Share
JSC TBC Bank	83.26%
Oikocredit, Ecumenical Development Co-operative Society U.A	10.97%
Individual Shareholders	5.77%

Source: JSC Bank Constanta, Annual Report, 2011

Table 21: ACLEDA Bank Plc. - Shareholder structure

Shareholder (as of June 03, 2011)	No. of Shares	Subscription Price (in USD)	Share
ACLEDA NGO	25,079,201	25,079,201	32.00%
ASA Plc.	14,890,775	14,890,775	19.00%
IFC	9,600,631	9,600,631	12.25%
JSH Asian Holdings Limited	9,600,631	9,600,631	12.25%
COFIBRED	9,600,631	9,600,631	12.25%
Triodos-Doen Foundation	3,415,104	3,415,104	4.36%
Triodos Fair Share Fund	3,386,912	3,386,912	4.32%
Triodos Microfinance Fund	2,798,615	2,798,615	3.57%
Total	78,372,500	78,372,500	100%

Source: ACLEDA Bank Plc, Annual Report 2011

Table 22: Nirdhan Bank - Shareholder structure

Shareholders (as of October 16, 2008)	No. of shares	Share	No. of members in the board	No. of shareholders
Group "A" Promoters	551.737	70%	5	23
Nirdhan NGO or	125.129	15.85%	1	1 (Institutional)
Grameen Trust, Bangladesh	40.766	5.16%		1 (Institutional)
Nabil Bank Limited	109.276	13.84%	1	1 (Institutional)
Himalayan Bank Limited	95.832	12.14%	1	1 (Institutional)
Everest Bank Limited	95.832	12.14%	1	1 (Institutional)
Individuals promoters	84.902	10.75%	1	18
Group "B" General public	237,544.24	30.00%	2	1.669
Independent Director			2	
Total		100%	9	1692

Source: Nirdhan Bank, Annual Report 2008

Table 23: Banco ADOPEM - Shareholder structure

Shareholder	Share	Paid-in Capital
(as of December 31, 2007)		(in USD)
ADOPEM NGO	69.57%	3,352,647
Local Shareholders	19.17%	923,973
International Shareholders (IFC and EIB)	11.26%	542,817

Source: Sumser (2008)

Table 24: Country comparison - Morocco, Bolivia and El Salvador as of 2010

Indicator	Morocco	Bolivia	El Salvador
Population	31,951,412	9,929,849	6,192,993
Population density (population/km^2)	70	9	289
Urban population rate	57	66	61
Rural population rate	43	34	39
Number of MFIs	10	27	18
GDP growth	3.70%	4.10%	1.40%
GDP per capita	2,850	1,810	3,380
Inflation rate	1.0%	2.5%	1.2%
Assault rate per 100,000 ('06)	186.00	54.20	75.90
Homicide rate	1.0% ('06)	28.0% ('06)	52.0% ('08)
Participation in organized criminal groups	0.5% ('06)		3.6% ('06)
Corruption rate ('06)	0.0%		0.3%

Source: World Bank Indicators, MIX dataset as of 02/2012, HEUNI, UNODC as of 2009

Table 25: PCB Bolivia - Loan portfolio characteristics

	2005		2006		2007		2008		2009		2010	
	No.	Vol.	No.	Vol.	No.	Vol.	No.	Vol.	No.	Vol.	No.	Vol.
Business loans/ total loan portfolio	76.6%	75.3%	90.6%	91.8%	90.3%	91.6%	90.3%	91.4%	89.5%	91.4%	86.5%	90.2%
Female borrowers/ business loan portfolio	52.8%	33.4%	51.7%	36.8%	52.4%	36.9%	51.6%	38.0%	50.4%	37.8%	46.5%	36.4%
PAR > 30 days/ business loan portfolio	3.5%	1.6%	3.2%	1.6%	2.9%	1.2%	2.2%	1.0%				
Maturity > 12 months/ business loan portfolio	64.3%	90.7%	50.8%	88.4%	56.1%	89.9%	57.4%	89.8%	59.8%	89.5%	64.2%	92.8%
Housing loans/ total loan portfolio	10.4%	18.3%	1.0%	1.7%	1.6%	2.1%	2.3%	2.3%	2.7%	2.4%	3.2%	3.1%
Consumer loans/ total loan portfolio	13.0%	6.4%	2.8%	2.3%	3.4%	2.2%	3.4%	2.1%	3.5%	1.8%	6.2%	2.6%

Source: Documents provided by the PCBs as of 07/2011

Table 26: PCB El Salvador - Loan portfolio characteristics

	2004		2005		2006		2007		2008		2009		2010	
	No.	Vol.	No.	Vol.	No.	Vol.	No.	Vol.	No.	Vol.	No.	Vol.	No.	Vol.
Business loans/ total loan portfolio	86.5%	75.7%	85.9%	75.3%	76.6%	89.1%	75.1%	89.3%	71.8%	89.7%	67.0%	89.7%	82.6%	93.7%
Female borrowers/ business loan portfolio	55.9%	40.0%	54.8%	41.4%	64.7%	40.4%	65.1%	38.0%	64.0%	33.1%	62.7%	30.6%	49.0%	25.2%
PAR > 30 days/ business loan portfolio	4.3%	2.1%	3.8%	1.9%	3.7%	1.7%	3.1%	1.6%	4.2%	2.3%				
Maturity > 12 months/ business loan portfolio	40.6%	81.0%	42.3%	81.7%	55.9%	89.7%	38.1%	84.9%	39.4%	87.1%	48.8%	90.5%	77.4%	93.7%
Housing loans/ total loan portfolio	13.4%	24.3%	14.0%	24.4%	2.6%	2.1%	3.0%	2.4%	3.1%	2.1%	3.2%	2.1%	4.3%	1.9%
Consumer loans/ total loan portfolio	0.0%	0.0%	0.0%	0.0%	0.0%	0.0%	0.0%	0.0%	0.0%	0.0%	0.0%	0.0%	0.0%	0.0%

Source: Documents provided by the PCBs as of 07/2011

Table 27: PCB Bolivia - Deposit characteristics

	2005		2006		2007		2008		2009		2010	
	No.	Vol.	No.	Vol.	No.	Vol.	No.	Vol.	No.	Vol.	No.	Vol.
Current accounts/ total accounts	0.0%	0.0%	0.0%	0.0%	0.0%	0.0%	0.1%	0.2%	0.3%	1.1%	0.5%	1.7%
Savings accounts/ total accounts	89.2%	16.3%	90.7%	15.0%	90.7%	15.0%	93.5%	29.3%	94.8%	32.1%	96.2%	33.5%
Term deposits accounts/ total accounts	10.8%	83.7%	9.3%	85.0%	9.3%	85.0%	6.4%	70.4%	4.9%	66.8%	3.4%	64.8%
Female depositors/ total accounts			52.5%	20.6%	52.5%	20.6%	56.3%	27.1%	56.0%	24.3%	55.5%	23.7%

Source: Documents provided by the PCBs as of 07/2011

Table 28: PCB El Salvador - Deposit characteristics

	2004		2005		2006		2007		2008		2009		2010	
	No.	Vol.	No.	Vol.	No.	Vol.	No.	Vol.	No.	Vol.	No.	Vol.	No.	Vol.
Current accounts/ total accounts	0.8%	1.2%	3.9%	3.7%	4.1%	5.7%	4.7%	7.8%	5.2%	6.6%	4.7%	9.4%	5.1%	15.8%
Savings accounts/ total accounts	88.7%	10.2%	76.1%	12.3%	69.3%	12.6%	66.9%	11.0%	65.2%	13.4%	63.6%	15.4%	62.5%	21.8%
Term deposits accounts/ total accounts	10.4%	88.5%	19.9%	84.1%	26.6%	81.6%	28.3%	81.3%	29.6%	80.0%	31.7%	75.2%	32.4%	62.4%
Female depositors/ total accounts					43.0%	19.9%	56.9%	16.0%	56.6%	20.1%	56.4%	23.9%	56.5%	24.7%

Source: Documents provided by the PCBs as of 07/2011

Table 29: FBPMC - Loan portfolio characteristics as of 09/2011 (in USD)

	Number	Volume
Individual loans	35,375	686,327,580
Group loans	174,628	1,633,609,000
Total	210,004	2,319,936,580
Individual loans over total loans	17%	30%
Group loans over total loans	83%	70%

	All loans		**Individual loans**	
Distribution by outstanding loan amount	Number	Volume	Number	Volume
up to 2,000	22	17,807	14	9,807
from 2,001 up to 10,000	249	475,348	27	43,848
from 10,001 up to 30,000	144,090	976,136,784	10,881	92,024,784
from 30,001 up to 50,000	58,325	1,026,197,046	19,344	368,063,046
from 50,001 up to 100,000	7,318	317,109,596	5,109	226,186,096
Distribution by Maturity				
up to 6 months	459	3,139,901	154	1,212,401
over 6 months to 12 months	74,878	473,937,983	3,977	41,104,483
over 12 months to 24 months	118,078	1,354,616,583	21,481	326,986,083
over 24 months to 36 months	12,148	303,189,891	6,116	162,166,391
over 36 months to 60 months	4,268	179,327,222	3,478	149,133,222
over 60 months	173	5,725,000	169	5,725,000
Distribution by frequency of instalments				
Weekly	14,017	185,738,744	1,101	20,906,244
Semi monthly	96,391	940,553,193	7,727	142,259,193
Every four weeks	97,993	1,167,638,237	24,945	497,155,737
Monthly	1,603	26,006,407	1,602	26,006,407
PAR>30 days	4,976	71,039,724	1,468	29,963,224
	2.37%	3.06%	4.15%	4.37%

Source: Documents provided by the FBPMC as of 10/2011

Table 30: ProCredit banks - Loan portfolio characteristics as of 07/2011 (in USD)

Distribution by outstanding loan amount	PCB Bolivia		PCB El Salvador	
up to 2,000	25,332	24,532,942	63,415	21,648,384
from 2,001 up to 10,000	29,906	142,971,956	18,639	60,330,697
from 10,001 up to 30,000	7,850	129,834,355		
from 30,001 up to 50,000	1,192	46,467,291	1,727	33,458,479
from 50,001 up to 100,000	531	36,184,757	163	11,563,433
from 100,001 up to 150,000	117	14,061,432	39	4,771,887
from 150,001 up to 500,000	85	19,427,385	65	14,756,904
from 500,001 up to 1,000,000	8	5,309,657	2	1,120,794
from 1,000,001 up to 1,500,000				
over 1,500,000	2	3,359,243		
	65,023	343,806,542	84,050	147,650,578
PAR>30 days	2,320	4,841,762	942	10,769,669
	3.57%	1.41%	1.12%	7.29%

Source: Documents provided by the PCBs as of 07/2011

Table 31: Microfinance banks in Bolivia and El Salvador as of 2010

	Assets	Deposits
BancoSol	585,816,714	420,063,364
FIE FFP	509,049,864	364,353,395
ProCredit Bank Bolivia	542,063,336	407,901,740
ProCredit Bank El Salvador	286,655,000	203,351,000

Source: MIX dataset as of 02/2012

Table 32: Bolivia - Development of bank deposits

	Bank deposits/GDP	GDP	No. of bank deposits
2005	0.3597957	9,549,196,302	3,435,759,768
2006	0.3333908	11,451,297,466	3,817,757,223
2007	0.3500999	13,120,517,443	4,593,491,845
2008	0.3669446	16,675,015,771	6,118,806,992
2009	0.3831874	17,339,992,191	6,644,466,524

Bank deposits growth of 93.39% from 2005 until 2009

Source: Database on Fin. Develop. and Structure 2010 and World Bank Indicators

Table 33: El Salvador - Development of bank deposits

	Bank deposits/GDP	GDP	No. of bank deposits
2005	0.3693902	17,093,800,000	6,314,282,201
2006	0.3603061	18,550,700,000	6,683,930,369
2007	0.3809814	20,104,900,000	7,659,592,949
2008	0.4013127	21,431,000,000	8,600,532,474
2009	0.4244423	20,661,000,000	8,769,402,360

Bank deposits growth of 38.88% from 2005 until 2009

Source: Database on Fin. Develop. and Structure 2010 and World Bank Indicators

Table 34: Gross loan portfolio over total assets of the 16 MFBs as of 12/2010

Name of the microfinance bank	Gross loan portfolio over total assets
ACLEDA	64.16%
ADOPEM	78.92%
Bancamia	88.50%
Banco ADEMI	83.88%
BancoSol	75.08%
BANEX ('09)	74.92%
CompartamosBanco	85.71%
D-Miro	85.59%
FIE FFP	81.97%
JSC Bank Constanta	81.19%
K-Rep	78.05%
MiBanco	82.94%
Caja Social BCSC	56.75%
Nirdhan	74.95%
Nerude Bank	82.73%
OBM	67.50%
PCB Bolivia	72.16%
PCB El Salvador	68.22%
Average	76.85%

Source: MIX dataset as of 01/2012

B Figures

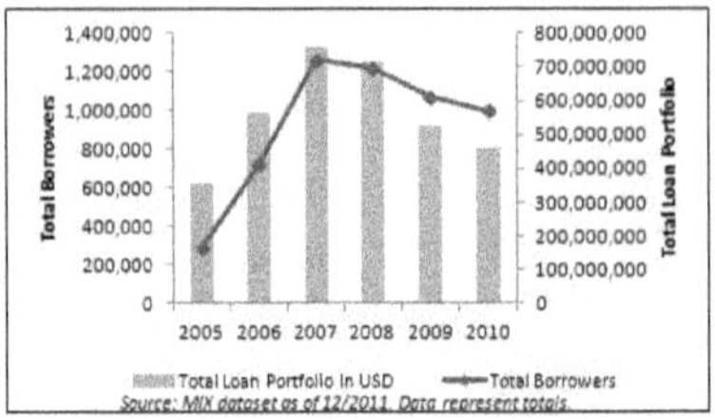

(a) Loan portfolio and borrowers

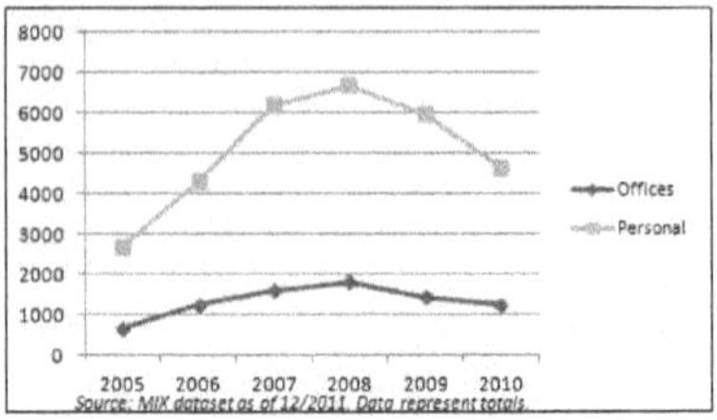

(b) Offices and personal

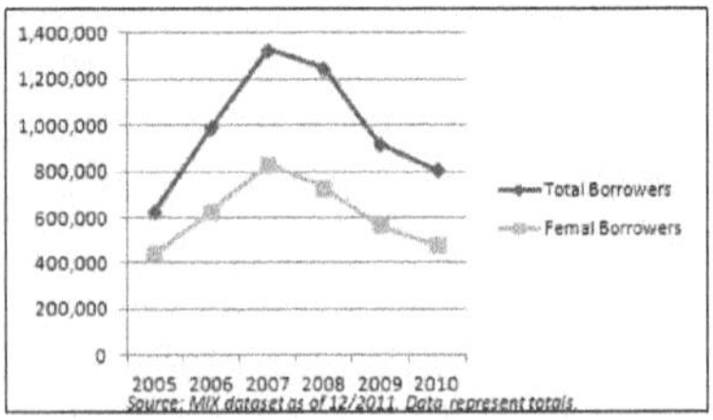

(c) Female borrowers

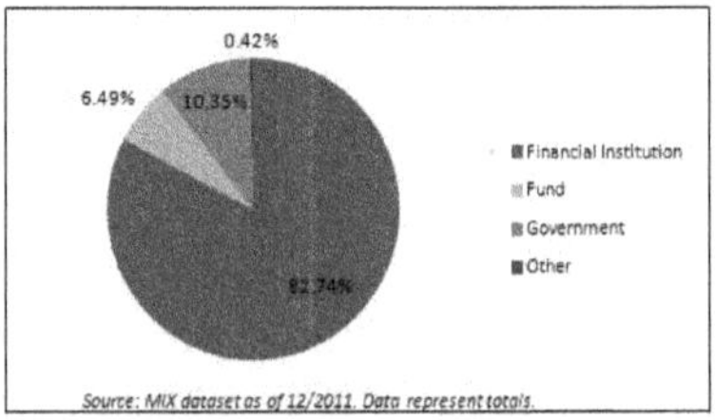

(d) Borrowings by type of lender

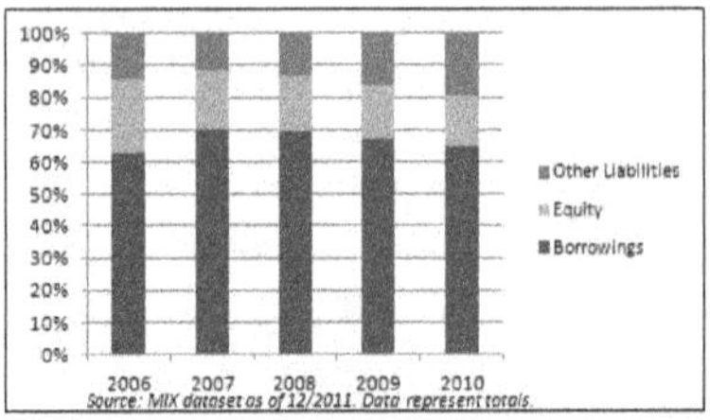

(e) Liabilities structure

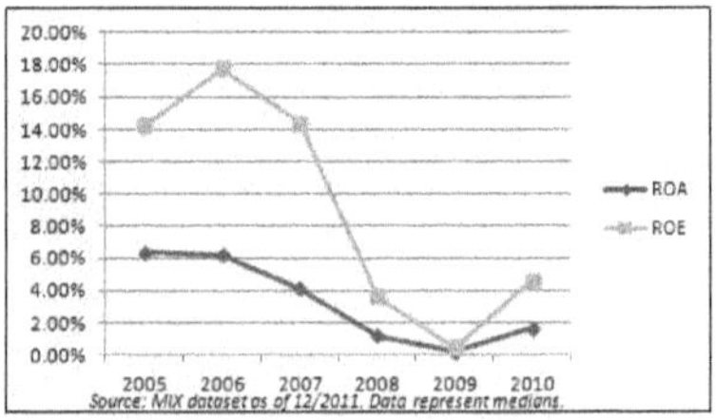

(f) Return on assets and return on equity

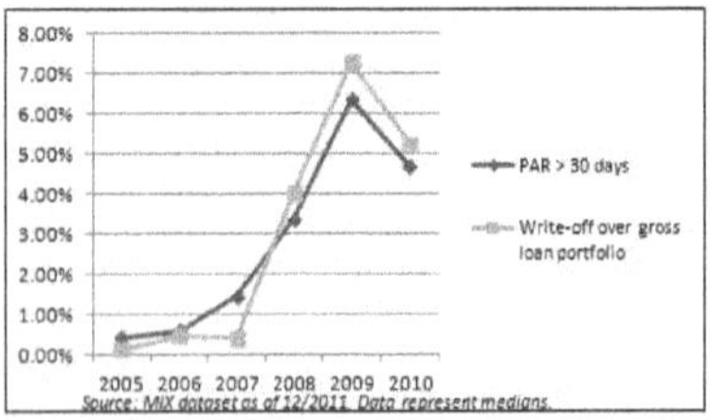

(g) Portfolio quality

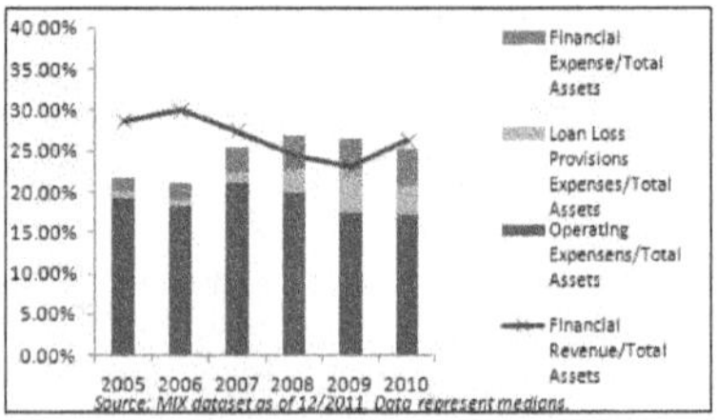

(h) Financial income and structure of expenses

Figure 1: Microfinance in Morocco

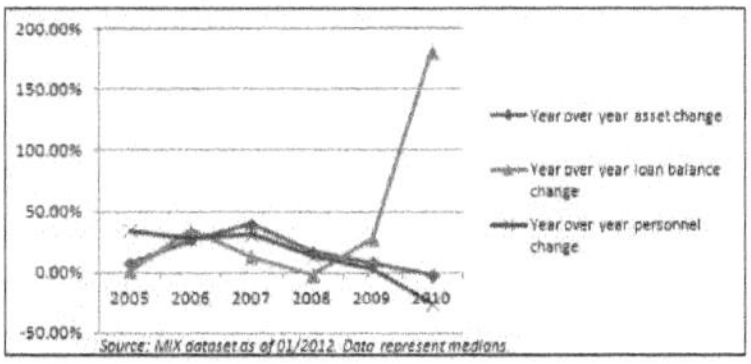

(a) ProCredit bank El Salvador - Size & outreach

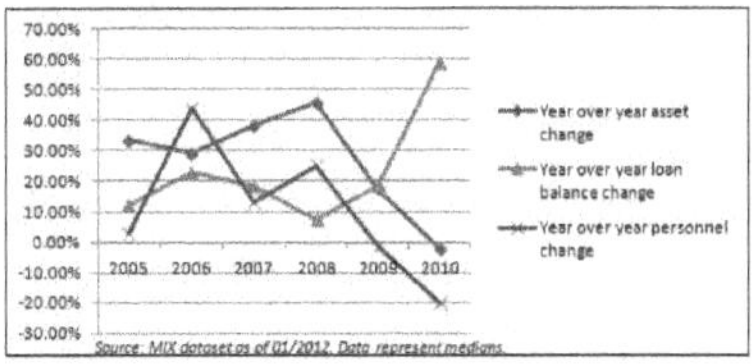

(b) ProCredit bank Bolivia - Size & outreach

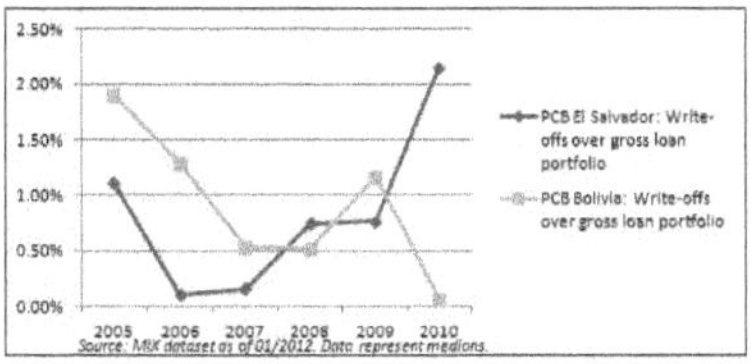

(c) PCBs - Portfolio quality (write-off ratio)

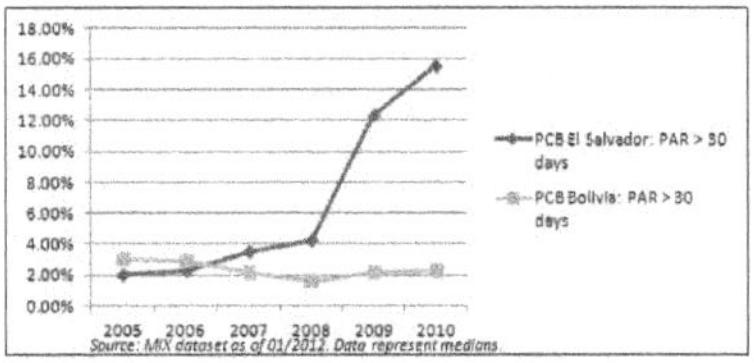

(d) PCBs - Portfolio quality (PAR>30 days)

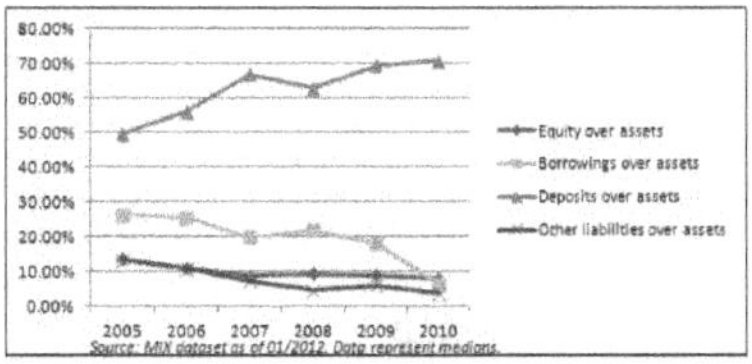

(e) ProCredit Bank El Salvador - Funding side

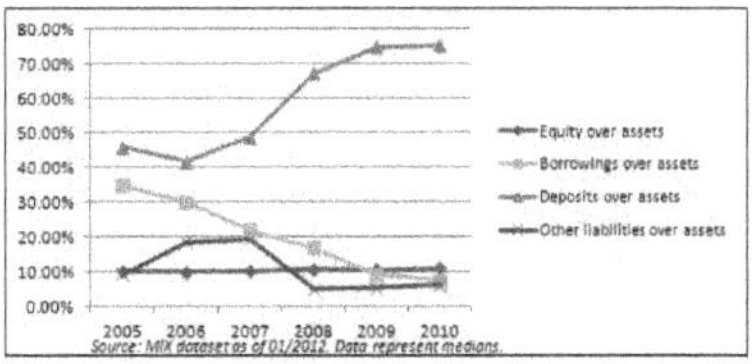

(f) ProCredit Bank Bolivia - Funding side

Figure 2: ProCredit banks in comparison

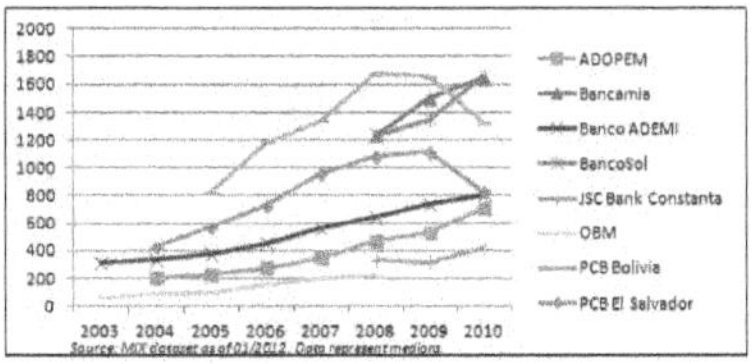

(a) Development of staff

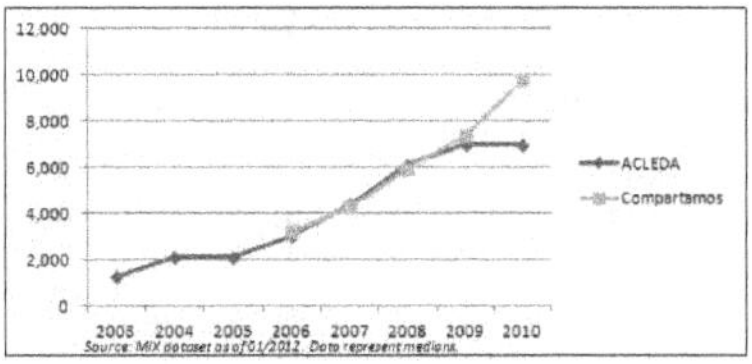

(b) Staff development - ACLEDA & Compartamos

Figure 3: Microfinance banks - Development of staff

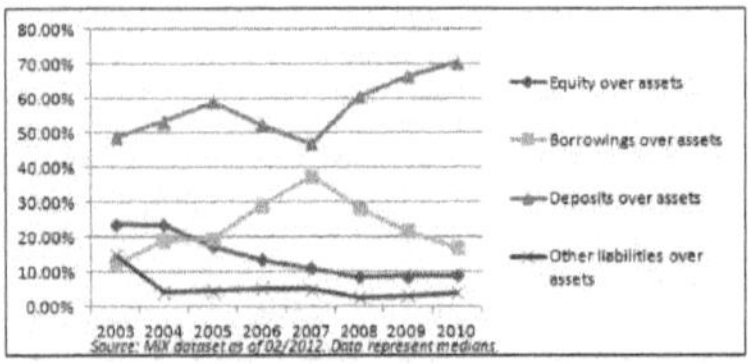

(a) MiBanco

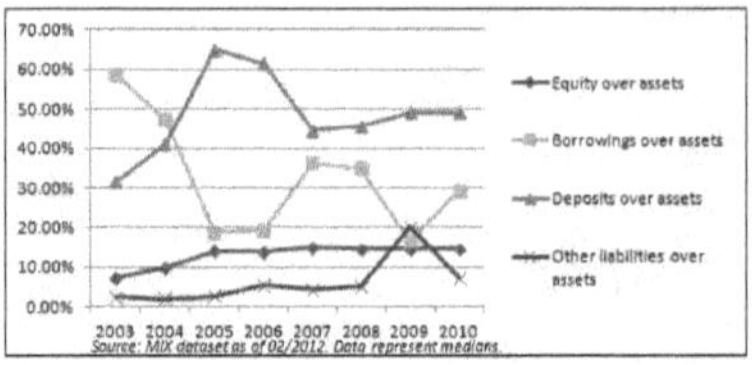

(b) Banco ADEMI

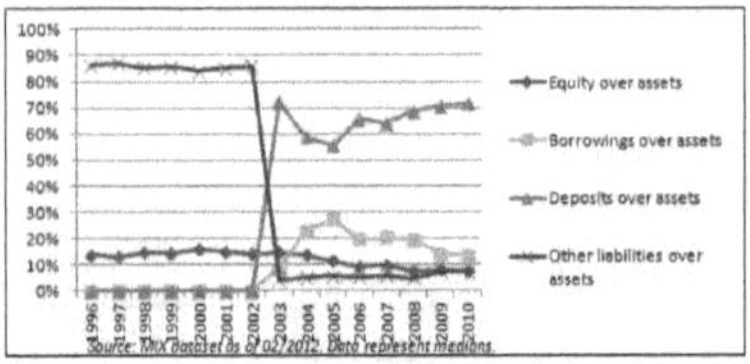

(c) BancoSol

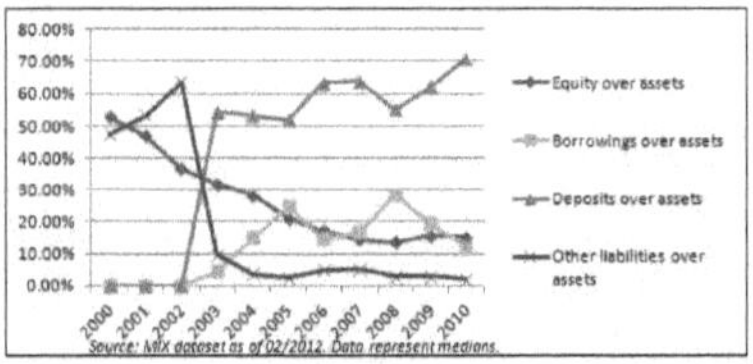

(d) K-Rep Bank

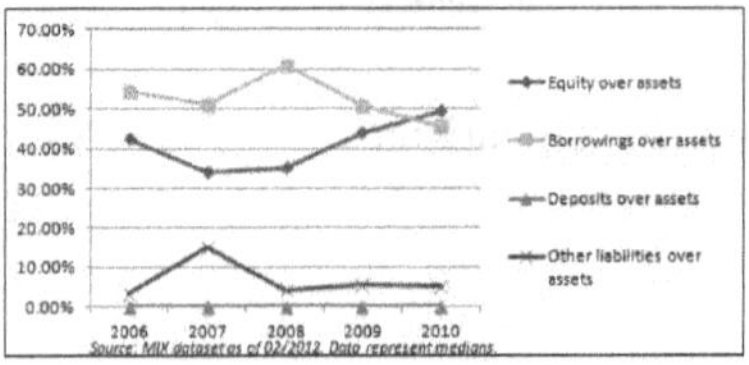

(e) Banco Compartamos

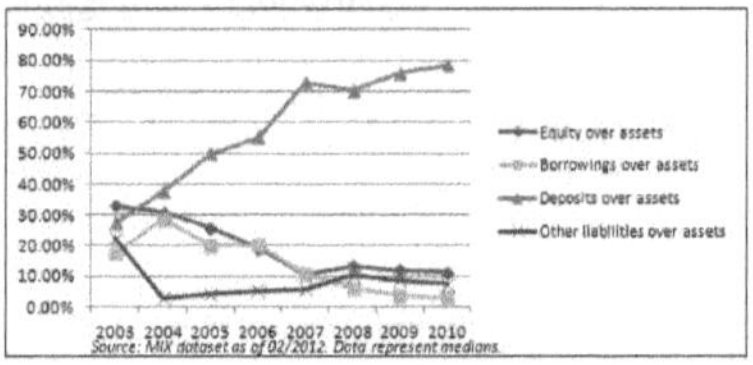

(f) ACLEDA Bank Plc.

Figure 4: Microfinance banks - Development of the funding side

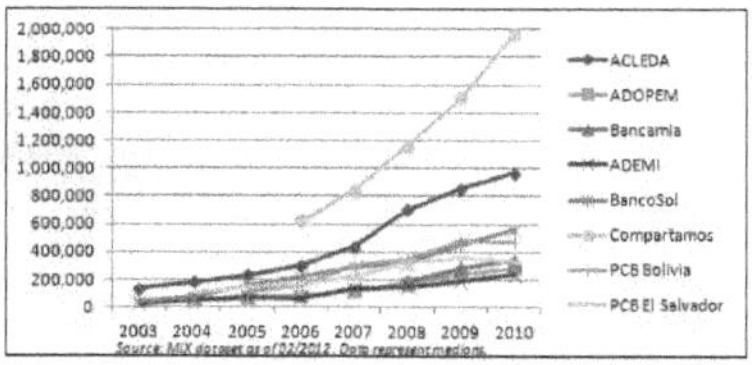

(a) Development of total clients

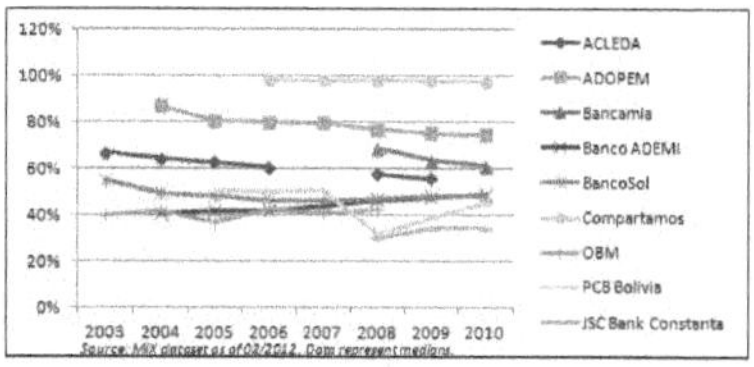

(b) Development of the share of female borrowers

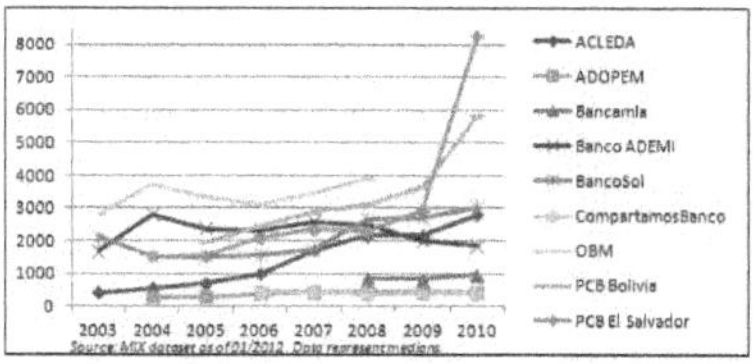

(c) Development of the average loan balance (in USD)

Figure 5: Microfinance banks - Development of outreach

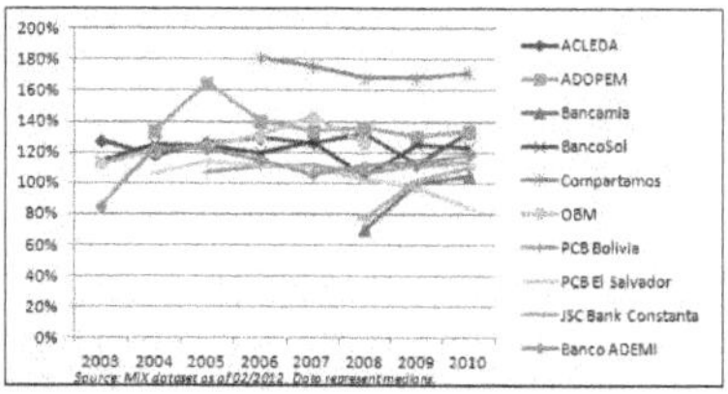

(a) Development of operational self-sustainability

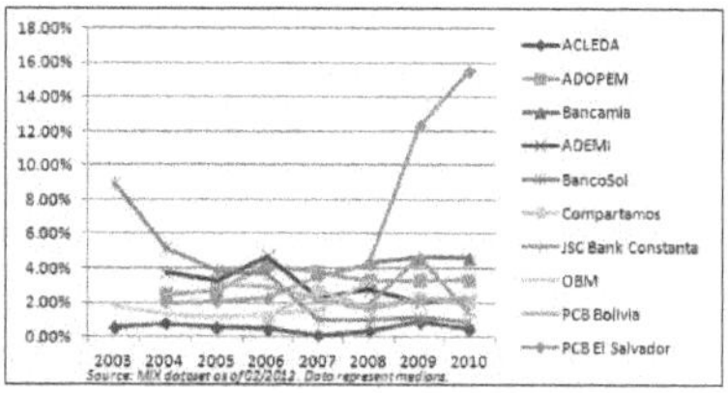

(b) Development of PAR>30 days

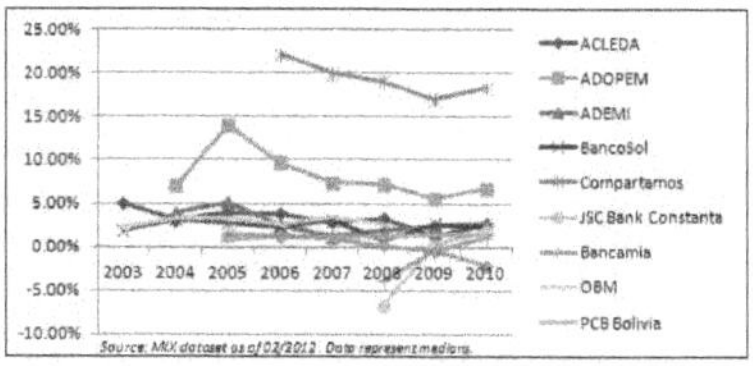

(c) Development of return on assets

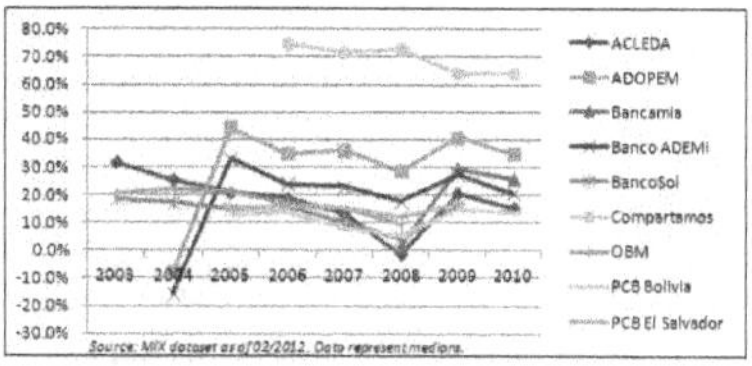

(d) Development of yield on gross loan portfolio

Figure 6: Microfinance banks - Development of financial performance

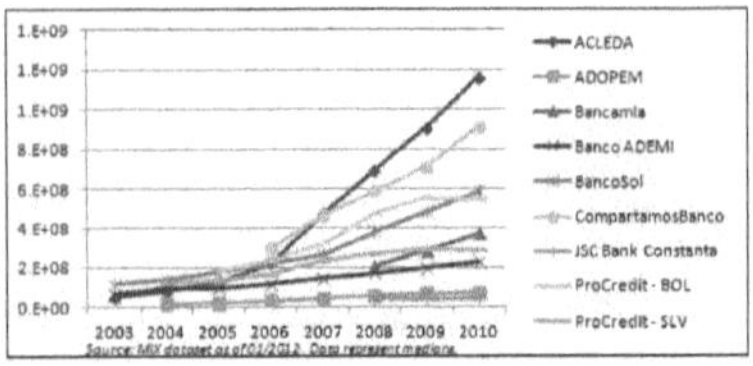

(a) Development of assets (in USD)

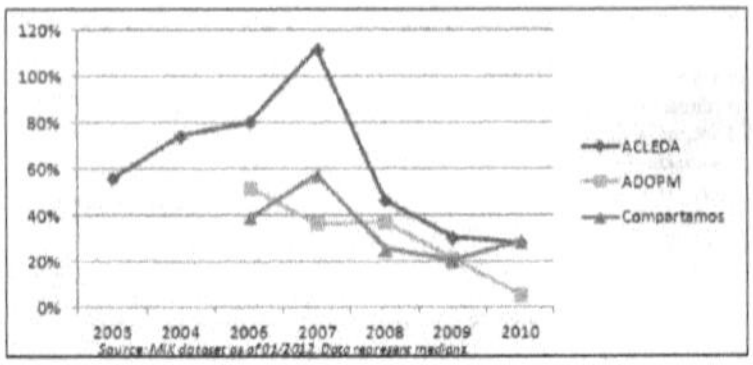

(b) Asset growth rates - ACELDA, ADOPEM & Compartamos

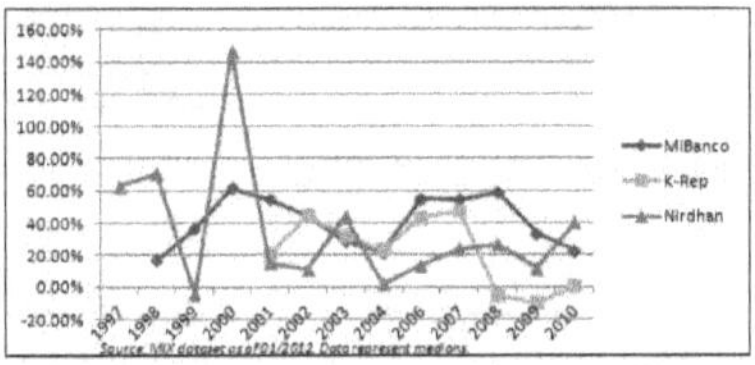

(c) Asset growth rates - MiBanco, K-Rep & Nirdhan

Figure 7: Microfinance banks - Development of assets

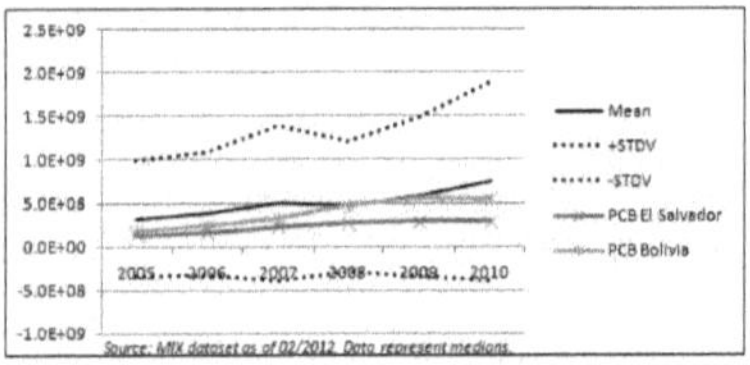

(a) Assets

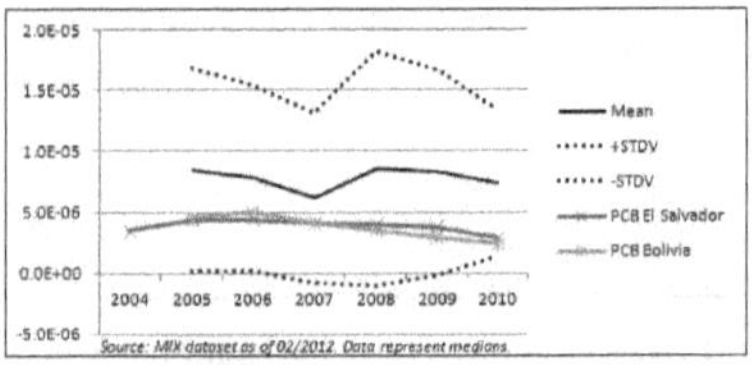

(b) Employees over assets

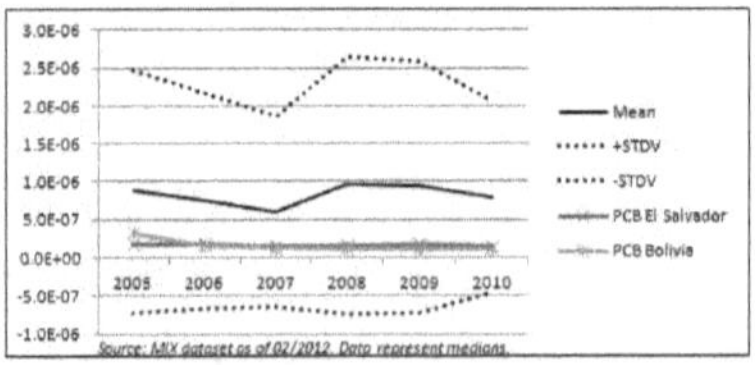

(c) Offices over assets

Figure 8: Comparative analysis of the MFBs in terms of institutional size

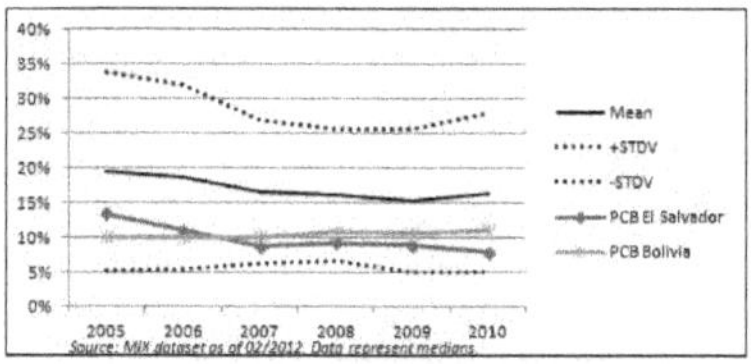

(a) Equity over assets

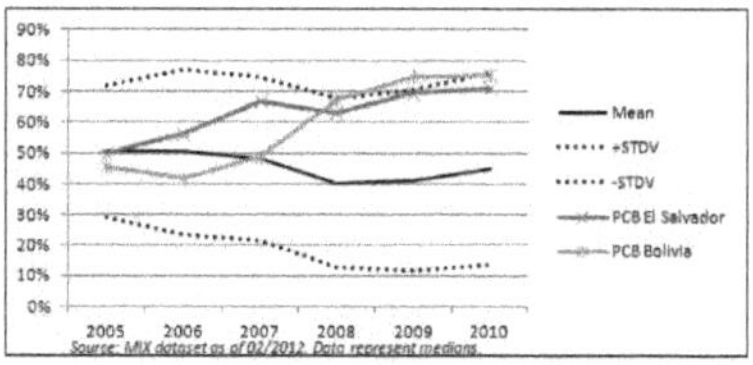

(b) Deposits over assets

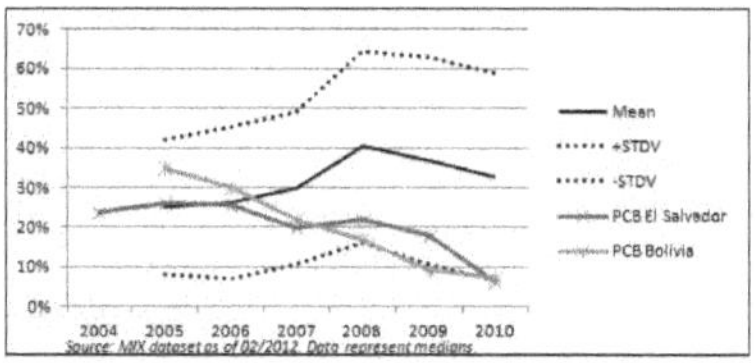

(c) Borrowings over assets

Figure 9: Comparative analysis of the MFBs in terms of the funding structure

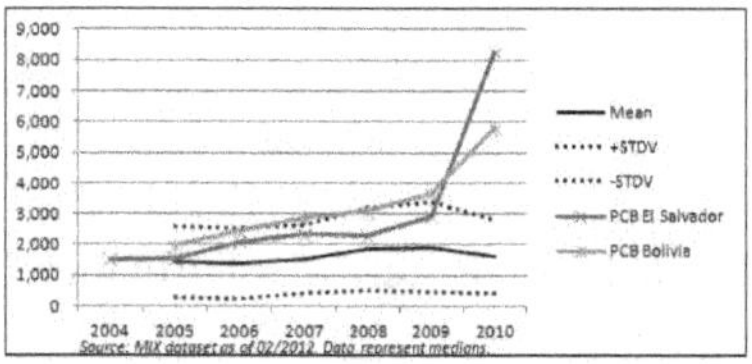

(a) Average loan balance per borrower

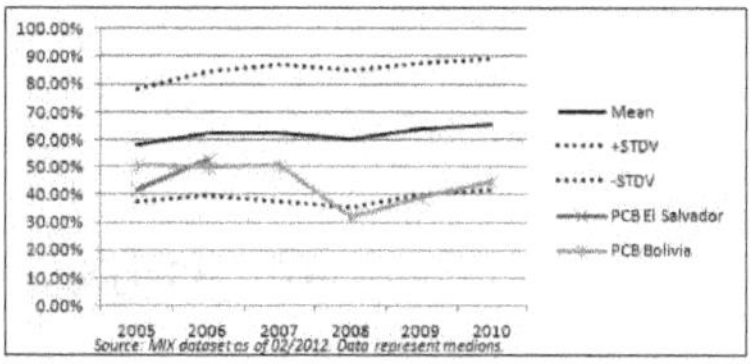

(b) Number of female borrowers/total borrowers

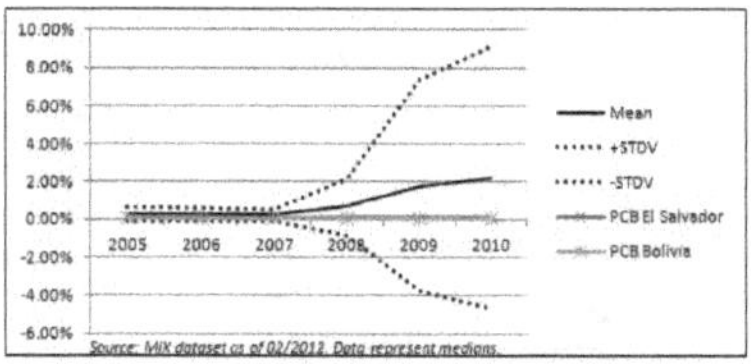

(c) Number of total clients over assets

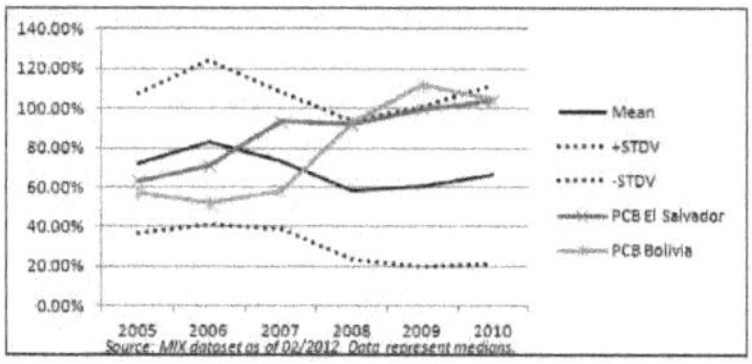

(d) Financial intermediation

Figure 10: Comparative analysis of the MFBs in terms of outreach and financial intermediation

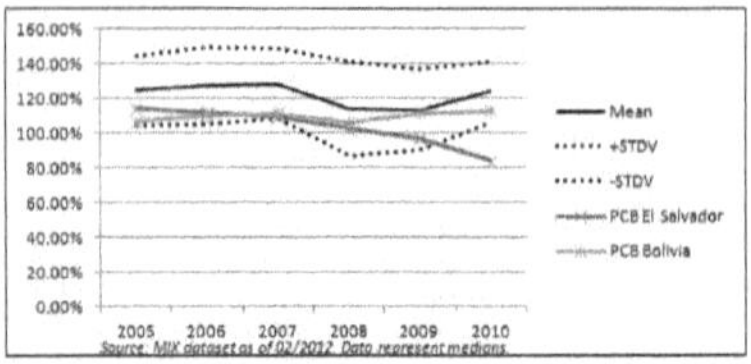

(a) Operational self-sufficiency

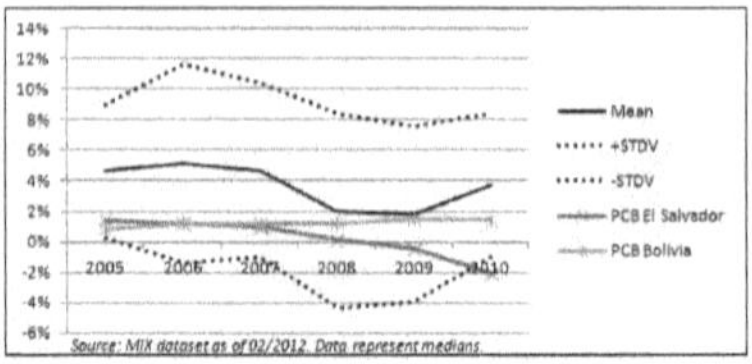

(b) Return on assets

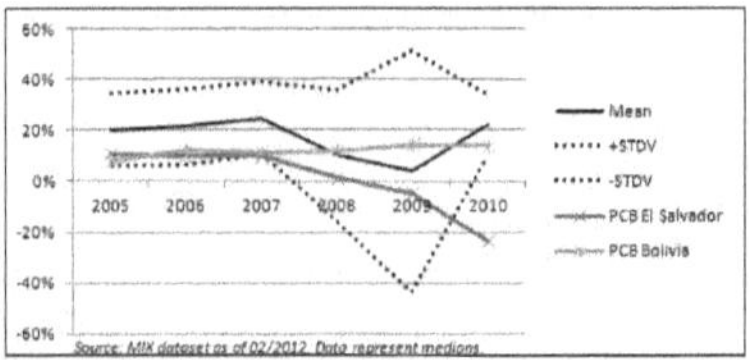

(c) Return on equity

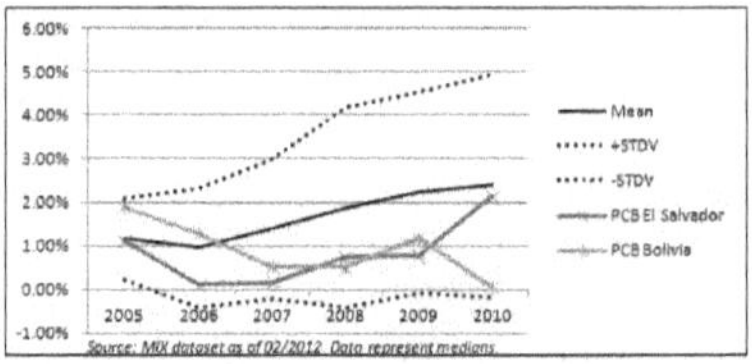

(d) Write-off ratio

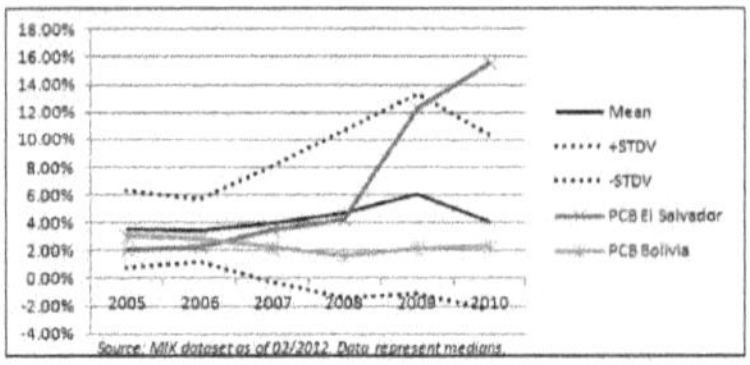

(e) Portfolio at risk > 30 days

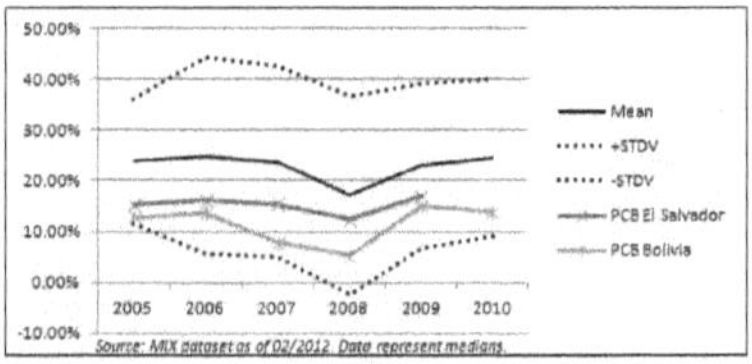

(f) Yield on gross loan portfolio (real)

Figure 11: Comparative analysis of the MFBs in terms of financial performance

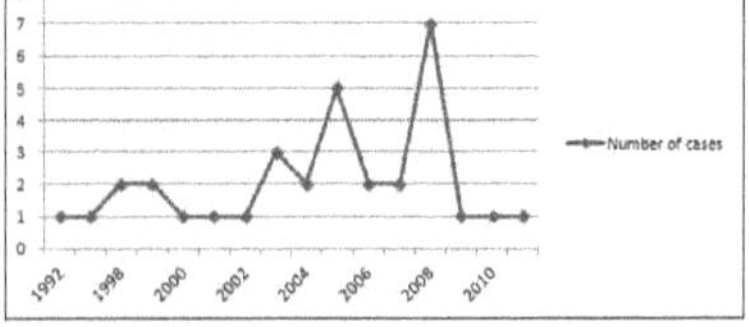

(a) Cases of transformation of MFIs into MFBs (own results)

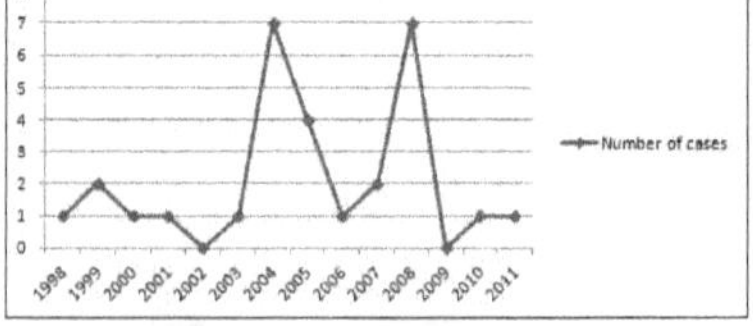

(b) Cases of transformation of MFIs into MFBs (results from MIXMarket organization)

Figure 12: Number of legal status transitions of microfinance institutions

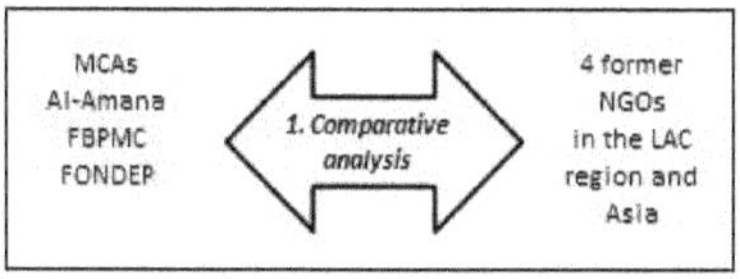

(a) First comparative analysis before the bank transformation in Chapter 4.1.1

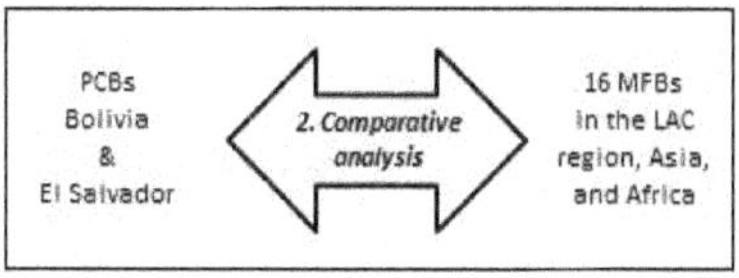

(b) Second comparative analysis after the bank transformation in Chapter 4.2.1

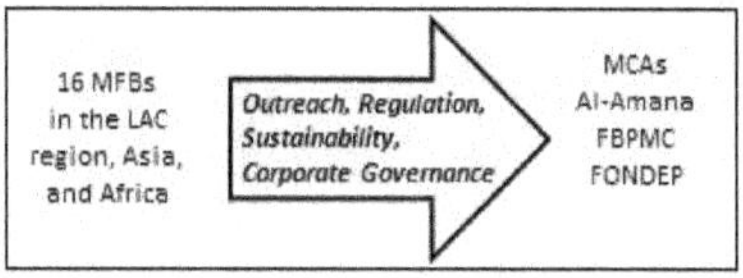

(c) Data application of the MFBs on the Moroccan MCAs in Chapter 4.2.2

Figure 13: Structure of the analysis part in this master's thesis

C Microfinance Infrastructure in Morocco

Supervisory authority:
Bank Al Maghrib (Moroccan central bank), www.bkam.ma
MFIs must regularly submit their outreach information, financial statements, and funding information to the BAM.

Microfinance specific legislation:
Microcredit Associations Law No. 18-97 promulgated on February 5, 1999
The 1999 Law No. 18-97 requires a specific legal status for MCAs, a lending limit of 50,000 MAD and financial sustainability after five years of existence MIXMarket (2010). The legal framework requests the institutions granting microcredits to justify their viability. Moreover, they are expected to produce a business plan, as well as a forecast of the necessary human and financial means relating to their development. Institutions which commit to these conditions obtain the agreement of the *Ministry of the Economy and Finances* to operate as a MCA. The law was amended by the law No. 58-03 in order to extend the field of intervention of MCAs. They could finance acquisitions, restore and extend social housing in favour of poor households, as well as enable the water support of their residences (Atallah and El Hyani, 2009; Reille and Lyman, 2005; FONDEP, 2011).

Network:

Fédération Nationale des Associations de Microcrédit (FNAM), www.fnam.ma

All permit-holding MCAs in Morocco are required to be members of an association. The FNAM was created in 2001 and revised its statutes in 2008. The Federation offers its support to the restructuring of the sector through the moderation of committees and working groups. Furthermore, it is a representative of the associations in dealings with relevant authorities. It also develops a code of conduct and other standards and resources for the sector (Atallah and El Hyani, 2009; MIXMarket, 2010; Reille and Lyman, 2005).

Credit bureau:

Informal credit bureau

Eight of twelve MCAs share information. The credit bureau was initiated by the 4 largest MCAs in 2007 and hosted at Al Amana.

credit bureau (under implementation)

A formal credit bureau is being considered with support from IFC and under the auspices of the BAM (MIXMarket, 2010; IMF, 2008; Reille and Lyman, 2005).

Development program:

Millennium Challenge Account: Microcredit/Financial Services project, www.app.ma

The objective of this project is to strengthen the promotion and development of MCAs to enable them to increase their outreach and efficiency in achieving their social mission (MIXMarket, 2010).

JAÏDA:

Investment Fund dedicated to the Moroccan microfinance industry, www.jaida.ma

JAÏDA facilitates financial access for MFIs by offering senior and subordinated debt. Its loan portfolio as of March 2010 was 384 million MAD ($46 million) Total disbursement: 544 million MAD ($65 million)(MIXMarket, 2010; Atallah and El Hyani, 2009).

D Profiles of Other Selected Transformed Microfinance Banks

Banco ADOPEM in Santa Domingo, Dominican Republic

The *Banco de Ahorro y Crédito* was created in 1982 and belongs to the Women's World Banking Network (Banco ADOPEM, 2008). Since its establishment in 1979, the network has been committed to microfinance and holds several affiliates around the world. Its members support low income female entrepreneurs and producers by enabling their financial access. Thus, female clients are able to expand their economic participation, assets and power (Harmeling and Austin, 2000). In the year 2005 ADOPEM began its operations as a savings and loan bank. The NGO ADOPEM still exists besides the banking institution. During its lifetime, ADOPEM benefits from several international development institutions such as the Inter-American Development Bank, GIZ (former GTZ), IFC, and EIB among others. ADOPEM tries to achieve a high level of operational efficiency. The institution wants to have a positive impact in the development of the country and be competitive in the long-term at the same time. The bank grants loans mainly to solidarity groups and to individuals. They grant agricultural, housing and consumer loans, as well as loans for abused women. Loan terms range between 4 to 36 months and they can be used for working capital or fixed investments purposes. Most of the clients are female borrowers who want to create their own business or strengthen their existing microenterprises (Banco ADOPEM, 2008; Sumser, 2008).

BANEX bank in Managua, Nicaragua

Banco del Exito was founded out of the former NGO FINDESA. FINDESA was created in January 1993 in Managua, Nicaragua and provided microfinance services. In 2002, the challenge of becoming a regulated financial institution was accomplished. The new limited company FINDESA started to be regulated by the banks' superintendence of Nicaragua. Four years later, FINDESA acquired the license to work as a bank and thus became BANEX. They provide short and long term financial services to micro, small, medium and large enterprises. Moreover, they operate in a profitable way respecting the principles of social responsibility (BANEX, 2010; CGAP, 2009). The BANEX Bank has operated only two years as a MFB. Due to the financial crisis, BANEX was liquidated in 2010 (Bédécarrats *et al.*, 2012). The banks' clients were microentrepreneurs that belong to the informal sector. Therefore, BANEX has designed a wide range of loan products adapted to this sector. Some of the products and services were revolving lines of credit (for microentrepreneurs that have more than one cancelled loan) and personal loans (consumer loans not related to their business). Furthermore, they have offered industrial loans (targeted to small, industrial entrepreneurs that are looking for capital to expand their company) and agricultural loans. Besides loans, BANEX has provided voluntary savings, insurance and fund transfer services (BANEX, 2010).

ACLEDA Bank in Phnom Penh, Cambodia

The ACLEDA bank was established as a National NGO for micro and small enterprise development. The NGO was supported by the UNDP and the ILO. It was called the ILO/UNDP project for social and economic rehabilitation by promoting the *Small Enterprise and Informal Sector Program*. The aim was to support local economic development by establishing an integrated small enterprises and informal sector program. Furthermore the sustainable provision of financial services to micro and small business entrepreneurs should contribute to the alleviation of poverty. ACLEDA's target groups were demobilized soldiers, handicapped persons, returned refugees, displaced persons, widows/widowers, and other war-affected people. They should have the possibility to start or expand a business and to generate income and employment. The NGO implemented a branch network by establishing 5 branches in 5 different provinces (out of 24) in Cambodia. At this point of time, they offered micro and small credits to business entrepreneurs, as well as non-financial services just as business management trainee programs and general support (ACLEDA Bank Plc, 2012). Some major product characteristics were:

Table 1: ACLEDA NGO - Loan products and requirements

	Micro Credit	Small Credit
Group member:	5 to 10 members	Individual small-scale entrepreneurs
Requirements:	Group guarantee	Collateral requirement, Proper business plan
Loan size:	\$25 to \$300 per member	from \$300 to \$25,000
Loan terms:	3 to 6 months	1 to 3 years (grace period for start-up)
Interest rate:	2% - 5% flat per month	10% to 18% flat per year

Source: Documents provided by ACLEDA Bank

In the years from 1993-1995, the ACLEDA NGO showed increasing numbers of active borrowers, as well as an expanding loan portfolio.

Table 2: ACLEDA NGO - Extensive growth in the first years of operation

	1993	1994	1995
Active borrowers:	1,475	2,344	6,539
Loan Outstanding (USD):	218,902	331,397	1,170,314

Source: Documents provided by ACLEDA Bank

In 1995, ACLEDA planned to restructure itself into a fully self-financing MFI which specialises in providing financial services to the lower segments of the market. Again, ACLEDA was supported by the two organizations UNDP/ILO (ILO/UNDP's project for *Alleviation of poverty through ACLEDA's financial services*). Therefore, the UNDP provided grant funding for technical assistance, capacity building and operational costs in the years of 1996 until 1997. In this period, ACLEDA was in its restructuring process to become a sustainable microfinance NGO. Later in 1998, a three-year program for transformation started with the assistance, e. g., from USAID, IFC and UNDP. It was completed with the granting of a specialized bank license in October 2000. In December 2003, ACLEDA Bank received its full commercial bank license and is named ACLEDA Bank Plc. Today, they are offering a wide range of products such as cash management, deposits, trade finance and electronic banking services (Source: Documents provided by ACLEDA Bank).

E MIX Market Glossary

Administrative Expense Ratio:

(Administrative Expense + Depreciation)/ Assets, average

Assets:

Total of all net asset accounts

Average Deposit Account Balance:

Deposits/ Number of Deposit Accounts

Average Deposit Balance per Depositor:

Deposits/ Number of Depositors

Average Outstanding Balance:

Loan Portfolio, Gross / Number of Loans Outstanding

Average Outstanding Balance / GNI per capita

Average Loan Balance per Borrower:

Loan Portfolio, Gross / Number of Active Borrowers

Average Loan Balance per Borrower/ GNI per capita

Personnel Expense / Personnel, average / GNI per capita

Bank:

A licensed financial intermediary regulated by a state banking supervisory agency. It may provide any of a number of financial services, including: deposit taking, lending, payment services, and money transfers.

Borrowings:

The total balance of funds borrowed by the MFI from investors, banks, donors or other lenders.

Capital / Asset Ratio:

Total Equity/ Total Assets

Cost per Borrower:

Operating Expense/ Number of Active Borrowers, average

Cost per Loan:

Operating Expense/ Number of Outstanding Loans, average

Debt / Equity Ratio:

Liabilities/ Equity

Deposits:

Total deposits, whether voluntary, compulsory, retail or institutional are presented under Deposits on the face of the balance sheet. This change means that the Total Deposits amount is higher than previously reported. Ratios, such as deposits-to-assets, are also impacted. This change brings microfinance reporting in line with the MFIs' own financial statements. Users may also view more detailed breakouts on deposits by reviewing the segments reported. Deposits are broken out according to the type of client and product. This additional break includes disclosures of voluntary vs. compulsory deposits, and retail vs. institutional deposits.

Deposits to Loans:

Deposits/ Loan Portfolio , gross. See also Data note for historical differences in treatment of deposits and the loan portfolio.

Deposits to Total Assets:

Deposits / Total Assets. See also Data note for historical differences in treatment of deposits.

Equity:

Total of all equity accounts, less any distributions.

Financial Expense:

These expenses will continue to be classified by associated liability, but are also broken down by type of expense (interest, fee) for each associated financial liability. Historical data from MIX Market does not offer a comparable level of detail in the income statement.

Financial Expense / Assets (%):

Financial Expense/ Assets, average

Financial Revenue:

Revenues from the loan portfolio and from other financial assets are broken out separately and by type of income (interest, fee). Historical data from MIX Market does not offer a comparable level of detail in the income statement.

Financial Revenue Ratio (%):

Financial Revenue/ Assets, average

Financial Intermediation:

This classification measures the extent to which an MFI intermediates between savers and borrowers, funding its assets through mobilized deposits.

Gains (losses):

As exchange and other gains (losses) from financial assets or liabilities have increased in value, the income statement now contains separate gain (loss) line items. Financial income and expense ratios may vary when compared with prior year results.

GNI per capita, Atlas method (current USD):

GNI per capita (formerly GNP per capita) is the gross national income, converted to U.S. dollars using the World Bank Atlas method, divided by the midyear population. GNI is the sum of value added by all resident producers plus any product taxes (less subsidies) not included in the valuation of output plus net receipts of primary income (compensation of employees and property income)from abroad. GNI, calculated in national currency, is usually converted to U.S. dollars at official exchange rates for comparisons across economies, although an alternative rate is used when the official exchange rate is judged to diverge by an exceptionally large margin from the rate actually applied in international transactions. To smooth fluctuations in prices and exchange rates, a special Atlas method of conversion is used by the World Bank.

Impairment Loss:

The non-cash expense calculated as a percentage of the value of the loan portfolio that is at risk of default. This value is used to create or increase the impairment loss allowance on the balance sheet.

Inflation Rate:

Indices shown for Consumer Prices are the most frequently used indicators of inflation and reflect changes in the cost of acquiring a fixed basket of goods and services by the average consumer. The percent changes are calculated from the index number series. Preference is given to series having wider geographical coverage and relating to all income groups, provided they are no less current than more narrowly defined series. The weights are usually derived from household expenditure surveys (which may be conducted infrequently). Other limitations might exist in terms of coverage of commodities for pricing, income groups, or their expenditure in the chosen index. The Laspeyres index formula is the most commonly used to calculate the changes in consumer prices.

Loan Loss Rate:

(Write-offs - Value of Loans Recovered)/ Loan Portfolio, gross, average

Loan Portfolio, gross:

All outstanding principals due for all outstanding client loans. This includes current, delinquent, and renegotiated loans, but not loans that have been written off. It does not include interest receivable. See also Data note for historical differences in treatment of the Loan Portfolio.

Loans:

Loan portfolio includes all loans made by the MFI, regardless of product or client type. This change means that total loan portfolio numbers are higher than previously reported. Ratios, such as loan portfolio assets or operating expense/loan portfolio are also impacted. This change brings microfinance reporting in line with the MFIs' own financial statements. Users may also view more detailed breakouts on loan portfolios by reviewing the segments reported. Loan portfolios are broken out according to the type of client and product, the economic sector being financed, lending methodology and other relevant segments. This additional breakout includes disclosure of microenterprise vs household and consumer financing as well as retail vs institutional lending.

Net Operating Income:

Financial Revenue - (Financial Expense + Impairment Loss + Operating Expense).

NGO:

An organization registered as a non profit for tax purposes or some other legal charter. Its financial services are usually more restricted, usually not including deposit taking. These institutions are typically not regulated by a banking supervisory agency.

Non-Bank Financial Institution:

An institution that provides similar services to those of a Bank, but is licensed under a separate category. The separate license may be due to lower capital requirements, to limitations on financial service offerings, or to supervision under a different state agency. In some countries this corresponds to a special category created for microfinance institutions.

Number of Active Borrowers:

The number of individuals or entities who currently have an outstanding loan balance with the MFI or are primarily responsible for repaying any portion of the Loan Portfolio, Gross. Individuals who have multiple loans with an MFI should be counted as a single borrower. See also Data note for historical differences in treatment of the Borrowers.

Number of Active Clients:

Number of individuals who are active borrowers and/or savers with the MFI. A person with more than just one such account (i.e. with a loan and a savings account) is counted as a single client in this measure.

Number of Deposit Accounts:

Number of any type of deposit account held by the MFI, whether voluntary or compulsory. See also Data note for historical differences in treatment of the Deposit Accounts.

Number of Depositors:

Number of clients with any type of deposit account, whether voluntary or compulsory. See also Data note for historical differences in treatment of Depositors.

Number of Loans Outstanding:

Number of loan accounts associated for any outstanding loan balance with the MFI and any portion of the Loan Portfolio. See also Data note for historical differences in treatment of the Borrowers.

Offices:

The number of staffed points of service and administrative sites used to deliver or support the delivery of financial services to microfinance clients.

Operating Expense:

Expenses related to operations, including all personnel expense, depreciation and amortization, and administrative expense.

Operating Expense / Assets (%):

Operating Expense/ Assets, average

Operating Expense / Loan Portfolio (%):

Operating Expense / Loan Portfolio, gross, average

Operational Self-Sufficiency (%):

Financial Revenue / (Financial Expense + Impairment Loss + Operating Expense)

Outreach:

Scale of outreach is measured as the total number of borrowers served.

Percent of Women Borrowers (%):

Number of Active Borrowers who are women / Number of Active Borrowers

Personnel:

Total number of staff members.

Personnel Expense:

All personnel expenses related to operations.

Personnel Expense / Assets (%):

Personnel Expense / Assets, average

Personnel Expense / Loan Portfolio (%):

Personnel Expense / Loan Portfolio, gross, average

Portfolio at Risk >(XX) days:

The value of all loans outstanding that have one or more instalments of principal past due more than (XX) days. This includes the entire unpaid principal balance, including both the past due and future instalments, but not accrued interest. It also includes loans that have been restructured or rescheduled.

Portfolio at Risk >30 days Ratio (%):

Portfolio at Risk >30 days/ Loan Portfolio, gross

Portfolio at Risk >90 days Ratio (%):

Portfolio at Risk >90 days/ Loan Portfolio, gross

Portfolio to Assets:

Loan Portfolio, gross/ Assets Profit Margin:

Net Operating Income/ Financial Revenue

Profit Status:

According to their registration, MFIs are classified as "not for profit" and "for profit" institutions.

Provision for Loan Impairment / Assets:

Impairment Loss/ Assets, average

Return on Assets (%):

(Net Operating Income, less Taxes)/ Assets, average

Return on Equity (%):

(Net Operating Income, less Taxes)/ Equity, average

Sustainability:

MFIs are grouped according to their level of financial self-sufficiency, representing their ability to cover all costs on an adjusted basis.

Taxes:

Includes all taxes paid on net income or other measure of profits as defined by local tax authorities. This item may also include any revenue tax. It excludes taxes related to employment of personnel, financial transactions, fixed-assets purchase or other value-added taxes.

Total Expense / Assets (%):

(Financial Expense + Impairment Loss + Operating Expense) / Assets, average

Write Off Ratio (%):

Write Offs / Loan Portfolio, gross, average

Write Offs:

Total amount of loans written off during the period. A write-off is an accounting procedure that removes the outstanding balance of the loan from the Loan Portfolio and from the Impairment Loss Allowance when these loans are recognized as non-collectable.

Yield on Gross Portfolio (real) (%):

(Yield on Gross Portfolio (nominal) - Inflation Rate)/ (1 + Inflation Rate)

UNIVERSITY MEETS MICROFINANCE

edited by PlaNet Finance Deutschland e.V.

ISSN 2190-2291

1 *Pim Engels*
Mission Drift in Microfinance
The Influence of Institutional and Country Risk Indicators on the Trade-Off between the Financial and Social Performance of Microfinance Institutions
ISBN 978-3-8382-0123-8

2 *Thilo Klein*
Microfinance 2.0
Group Formation and Repayment Performance in Online Lending Platforms During the US Credit Crunch
ISBN 978-3-8382-0118-4

3 *Saikumar C. Bharamappanavara*
The Performance Of Microcredit Organisations
A Comparative Perspective
ISBN 978-3-8382-0121-4

4 *Oliver Rogall*
Microfinance and Vulnerability to Poverty
The Evidence from Rural Households in Cambodia
ISBN 978-3-8382-0237-2

5 *Maria Cristina De Lorenzo*
Microfinance Investment Funds: An analysis of profitability
ISBN 978-3-8382-0251-8

6 *Sascha Huijsman*
The Impact of the Current Economic and Financial Crisis on Microfinance
ISBN 978-3-8382-0235-8

7 *Funmilayo A. Akinosi, Daniel Nordlund, Alejandro Turbay*
Sustainable Microfinance
Redefining the Socio-Economic Mission in Microfinance
ISBN 978-3-8382-0334-8

8 *Anna Custers*
Furthering Financial Literacy
Experimental Evidence from a Financial Literacy Training Programme for Microfinance Clients in Bhopal, India
ISBN 978-3-8382-0337-9

9 *Thilo Klein*
Why Do India's Urban Poor Choose to Go Private?
Health Policy Simulations in Slums of Hyderabad
ISBN 978-3-8382-0238-9

Sie haben die Wahl:

Bestellen Sie die Schriftenreihe
University Meets Microfinance
einzeln oder im **Abonnement**

per E-Mail: vertrieb@ibidem-verlag.de | per Fax (0511/262 2201)
als Brief (*ibidem*-Verlag | Leuschnerstr. 40 | 30457 Hannover)

Bestellformular

❒ Ich abonniere die Schriftenreihe *University Meets Microfinance* ab Band # ____

❒ Ich bestelle die folgenden Bände der Schriftenreihe *University Meets Microfinance*
____; ____; ____; ____; ____; ____; ____; ____; ____; ____

Lieferanschrift:

Vorname, Name ....

Anschrift ....

E-Mail.. | Tel.: ....

Datum .... | Unterschrift ....

Ihre Abonnement-Vorteile im Überblick:

- Sie erhalten jedes Buch der Schriftenreihe pünktlich zum Erscheinungstermin – immer aktuell, ohne weitere Bestellung durch Sie.
- Das Abonnement ist jederzeit kündbar.
- Die Lieferung ist innerhalb Deutschlands versandkostenfrei.
- Bei Nichtgefallen können Sie jedes Buch innerhalb von 14 Tagen an uns zurücksenden.

***ibidem*-Verlag**
Melchiorstr. 15
D-70439 Stuttgart
info@ibidem-verlag.de

www.ibidem-verlag.de
www.ibidem.eu
www.edition-noema.de
www.autorenbetreuung.de

www.ingramcontent.com/pod-product-compliance
Lightning Source LLC
Chambersburg PA
CBHW070405200326
41518CB00011B/2068
9783838204949